An Italian Pantry

Pasta

Fabrizio Ungaro

An Italian Pantry

McRae Books

Also available in
"An Italian Pantry":

OLIVE OIL

CHEESE

DELI MEATS

First published in 2002 by
McRae Books Srl
Via de' Rustici, 5,
50122 Florence, Italy

ISBN 88-88166-17-3

This book was conceived, edited and designed by
McRae Books Srl, Florence, Italy.

Publishers: Anne McRae, Marco Nardi
Text: Fabrizio Ungaro
Photography: Marco Lanza, Walter Mericchi
Set Design: Rosalba Gioffrè
Design: Marco Nardi
Layout: Adriano Nardi, Laura Ottina
Translation from the Italian: Marilena Cairns
Editing: Anne McRae, Laura Ottina, Anne Charlish

2 4 6 8 10 9 7 5 3 1

Color separations: Fotolito Toscana, Florence, Italy
Printed and bound in Italy by Artegrafica

Contents

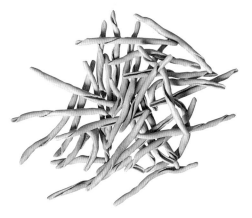

Introduction

Above: Advertising and marketing budgets for pasta have increased greatly in recent years, as pasta has become more and more popular. In Italy, where pasta has been a staple for many years, there are some charming ads dating from early in the 20th century, such as this one showing a baby St. George mounted on a pasta steed. (Courtesy of the Barilla Archive, Parma)

Below: No one quite knows exactly how many pasta shapes there are today. New ones are invented all the time and old ones fade away, while regional variations on the classic shapes continue to prosper. These thick wheel shapes are known as "crazy wheels."

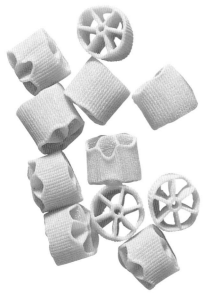

Italian food is still the most popular "ethnic cuisine" in North America and many parts of Europe, and pasta remains its flagship dish. According to *The American Pasta Report*, a survey commissioned in the United States in 2000, pasta consumption is still increasing as more and more people come to appreciate its unique combination of superb taste, versatility, nutritional value, and convenience.

Italy is the largest pasta producer in the world today, with more than 3 million tons produced each year, one-third of which is exported, mainly to Germany, the United States, and France. Not surprisingly, Italians lead the world in pasta consumption, tucking away an average of 62 lb (28 kg) each per year. What is striking, underlining this versatile food's international appeal, is that many other countries are catching up. Venezuelans and Tunisians consume an average of about 26 lb (12 kg) each. They are followed by Chile, at 22 lb (10 kg), the USA, with 20 lb (9 kg), and Canada and Germany at around 11 lb (5 kg) per head.

There are many reasons why pasta has become so popular in recent years. Firstly, research by food nutritionists has shown that it is a healthy food. Pasta is a good source of minerals such as iron, potassium, and phosphorus, and is rich in vitamins B1 and B2. It has even more vitamins and minerals when served with tomato or other vegetable sauces, and can also be a good source of protein when served with delicious meat or seafood sauces and sprinkled with freshly grated Parmesan or Pecorino cheese. Pasta is very easy to digest, making it an ideal food for people of all ages and constitutions. With about 356 calories per 100 grams, pasta is packed with energy. Eaten in moderate quantities with a judicious amount of sauce, it is not fattening.

Beyond the health aspects, pasta is popular because it is the ultimate convenience food. It is cheap to buy and can be stored for months before use. Pasta is easy and quick to prepare; a nutritious pasta salad, for instance, can be prepared in the time it takes to cook the pasta. Fresh tomatoes, garlic, salad greens, cheese, capers, olives, and other ingredients can be chopped while it cooks. Many vegetable sauces can also be prepared as the pasta itself cooks.

Versatility is another of pasta's virtues. In summer, a cool pasta salad makes a wonderful starter at dinner, a nutritious lunch, or a great barbecue or picnic food. In winter, hearty pasta soups and baked pasta dishes make warming meals for the whole family. Boiled fresh, filled, or dried pasta with meat or vegetable sauces are good all year round on any occasion.

Left: Price sticker for Barilla pasta, dating to 1927. (Courtesy of the Barilla Archive, Parma)

Below: This photo shows pasta being made in Naples at the beginning of the 20th century. (Courtesy of Barilla the Archive, Parma) The mechanization process was gradual, with Genoa and Naples becoming the manufacturing and export capitals for macaroni, vermicelli, and lasagne in the 19th century. The production of both fresh and dried pasta was still mainly homemade and manual, and until the middle of the 18th century, the bran and water mixture was kneaded by hand or foot. The pasta was dried out outside in the sun or in indoor drying chambers.

A Short History of Pasta

Above: European merchants returning from the East during the late Middle Ages. The famous story that it was Marco Polo who, in 1296, first brought pasta to Italy on return from his travels, is no longer taken seriously. Food historians have shown that there were centers of pasta production in Italy well before this date, especially in Sicily and Sardinia.

The Romans used wheat flour to make bread, both leavened and unleavened, while durum wheat flour was used to make pappe (bread soups) and puls (porridge-like mush). Before the Romans, the Etruscans are also thought to have prepared some kind of pasta. A fresco in an Etruscan tomb at Cerveteri is thought to show a pasta cutter very similar to these 18th and 19th century ones below. (Courtesy of the Barilla Archive, Parma)

There are almost as many theories concerning the origins of pasta as there are ways to serve it! The subject is still controversial and practically everyone, from China to Europe, has been credited with its invention over the centuries, including the Etruscans, Greeks, Romans, Arabs, Russians, and Chinese. Recent studies suggest that pasta, linked as it is to the cultivation of wheat and the production of flour, was invented and developed separately in the areas where cereals were grown.

The Romans grew wheat from the 5th century BC onward although they did not produce pasta as we know it, despite having the necessary technology. The Roman term *lagana*, of Greek origin, is thought to mean something similar in ingredients and shape, but not in preparation, to lasagne. Roman *lagana* is the first recorded example of dough that is kneaded and rolled out into sheets, but they were then cooked in oil or baked in the oven like unleavened bread. Galeno, a 2nd century Greek doctor, uses another term, *tria*, also of Greek origin, to refer to mixtures of flour and water, of which *lagana* seem to be a variant. The shape and use of *tria* are not clear, but it is certain that the term (*itryya*) was used in medieval times by the Arabs, who played a key role in spreading the early technology for drying pasta to Sicily and the rest of the Mediterranean. The Arab geographer, Al Idris, uses the term *tria* in 1154 to indicate unleavened strands of pasta which were produced in large quantities at Trabia, in Sicily, and exported to Calabria and other parts of the Mediterranean. Sicily soon became a major producer of dried pasta, while medieval chronicles reveal that the consumption of fresh pasta was spreading in northern Italy. In the 12th century, macaroni, later mentioned in Boccaccio's *Decameron*, makes its first appearance and during the 13th and 14th centuries many new types of pasta are recorded, including vermicelli, ravioli, tortelli, fidelli, and tagliatelle. Just how important pasta consumption was by 1500 is evident in notary deeds and customs documents, and from price fixing edicts, such as those issued in Milan in 1421, Palermo in 1501, and Naples in 1509. At this time too, pasta-making became a recognized trade. The first guilds of fresh pasta-makers appeared in the 14th century. They included the *lasagnari* in Florence (1311), the *vermicellari* in Naples (1579), and the *fidelari* in Genoa (1574).

In the 15th and 16th centuries recipes for fresh pasta began to appear in cook books and gastronomic treatises. Bartolomeo Scappi (1474) and Cristofero da Messisbugo (1548) recorded very well-cooked pasta dishes, that were often served with sugar and spices. These recipes were aimed at the upper classes, who preferred fresh pasta, especially the stuffed varieties.

With the advent of the first steam machinery, hydraulic presses, and then electricity, dried pasta manufacturing underwent a major revolution. The first machine capable of carrying out all stages of the production process – grinding, kneading, rolling, drying out, cooling down, and packaging, was patented in 1933. Since then, industrial pasta making has not looked back and pasta production increases each year.

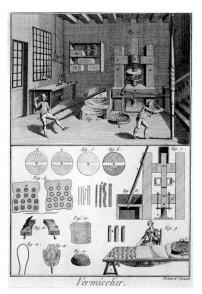

In the 17th century, there were so many vermicellari shops (like the one shown here) that, in a Papal bull of 1641, Urban VIII imposed a minimum distance of 79 feet (24 meters) between one shop and the next in an attempt to regulate pasta trading. (Courtesy of the Barilla Archive, Parma)

Right: One of the earliest rolling mills, used to crush the grain to make pasta, dating to 1890. (Courtesy of the Barilla Archive, Parma)

Types of Pasta

Above: Advertisement for pasta made by manufacturer Barilla (1927). (Courtesy of the Barilla Archive, Parma)

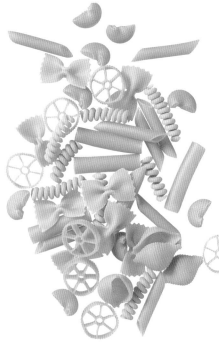

Below: Short pasta, perhaps more than any other kind, deserves the name "ingenious pasta," as dried manufactured pasta, artfully rolled out in the first industrial pasta factories, was called in 18th century Naples.

Italy is the only country in the world where two different pasta traditions developed at the same time. These were dried, durum (hard) wheat pasta, and fresh, soft wheat pasta. Even though far less fresh pasta is produced than dried (about 10 percent of total production), traditional Italian cuisine concentrated almost exclusively on fresh pasta for centuries, snubbing the dried variety as the staple food of poor people in Naples. This trend only began to change in the 20th century.

Short Pasta

Dried, durum wheat pasta now represents about 90 percent of all pasta made in Italy, and about 65 percent of this figure is made up of short pasta, making it the most popular type with consumers. The conquest by dried pasta, firstly of Italian tables and then of the global market, is a relatively recent occurrence which has imposed the Italian way of cooking and eating pasta *"al dente"* (literally "firm to the bite") on the world. This is the same pasta which, from the 18th century onward, established itself in Naples, earning that city the nickname of "the macaroni capital." Short pasta spread to the rest of Italy after the country was unified in 1861. Created to be served with thicker sauces, short pasta is now available in hundreds of shapes: flat, such as *farfalle* and *stricchetti*; twisted, like *eliche, fusilli,* and *gemelli*; tubular, obliquely cut like *penne,* or cut straight like *rigatoni*; and imaginative, like *ruote* (wheels), *gomiti* (elbows), and *lumache* (snails). Short pasta shapes vary greatly in size, from $1/4$-in (6-mm) *pennine* to 4-in (10-cm) *cannelloni*. Externally, short pasta is either smooth or ridged. There are also some regional specialities that are the pride of Italian pasta making: Apulian *orecchiette* (little ears), Sardinian *malloreddus* (small gnocchi-shaped pasta) and Valtellinese *pizzocheri* (short, broad, brownish-grey noodles).

Pastine (Soup Pasta)

Made from durum wheat flour or soft wheat flour with eggs, tiny soup pasta shapes were created to substitute the wheat which was traditionally used to give substance to meat and vegetable soups and stocks. It was probably one of the earliest types of dried pasta, since it kept well, was quick and easy to cook, and suitable for trading, even over long distances. In medieval Arabian cook books, the term *fidaws* is used to indicate small pasta shaped like kernels of grain. These are thought to have originated in the Arabian-controlled areas of Spain. The only pasta in use in Spain and other parts of the Mediterranean, it was not widespread in Italy until the 18th century, although there are a few recipes in cook books and treatises on cooking dating from the 15th and 16th centuries.

Soup pasta is now available in a wide variety of shapes. The smallest are tiny seed or grain shapes which are served in clear vegetable or meat soups (bouillon). The larger shapes, which are often hollow or ridged, are ideal for thicker vegetable soups and stocks made with pulses, such as beans, garbanzo beans (chickpeas), and lentils. They are widely used in regional dishes.

Long Pasta

Long pasta shapes can be either fresh or dried. Both are of ancient origin, although they are believed to come from two different traditions. Fresh long pasta is linked to the preparation of a sheet of pasta which was loosely rolled then cut to make flat *tagliarini* or *formentini*. Dried long pasta involved the preparation of little rolls of dough which were shaped by hand to make threads or round *vermicelli* (little worms), or perforated to make *macaroni*, which were then dried in the sun.

Today, most long pasta is made from durum wheat and dried, but there are also some dried egg pastas. Long pasta shapes range in diameter from about $^1/_{20}$ in (1 mm) (*fidelini*)

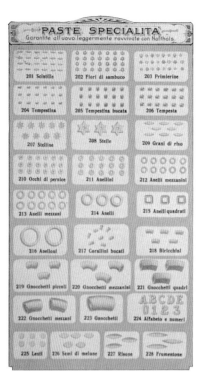

Above: The variety of soup pasta shapes available is nothing new. This is a page from Barilla's 1916 catalog. (Courtesy of the Barilla Archive, Parma)

Below: Spaghetti, and the slightly thinner, spaghettini. This is still the most popular type of pasta in Italy and probably the best known pasta shape in the world.

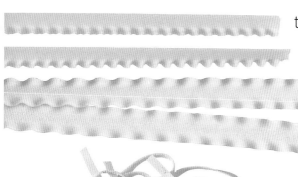

to ¹/₂ in (1 cm) (*ziti*). Long pasta can be either whole (*vermicelli*) or hollow (*bucatini*), with a round (*spaghetti*), elliptical (*linguine*), or flat (*fettuccine*) cross-section. It can be preserved in nests or tangled piles (*capelli d'angelo*), and have either smooth (*lasagne*) or curled (*mafaldine*) edges. Latian *bucatini*, Neapolitan *ziti*, and Genoese *trenette* are typical regional long pastas.

Special Pasta

In recent years, the pasta market has exploded with new shapes, colors, and flavors that have little in common with traditional pasta. The majority of these special pastas are not made in Italy and most of those that are, are destined for exportation. Coloring and flavoring of pasta does, however, have distant origins. From medieval times up until the end of the 17th century, saffron was used to color pasta, with some recipes suggesting the addition of rose water as well. Saffron is still used today in the traditional recipe for *malloreddus* (Sardinian gnocchetti). The use of spices and colorings in the past was also due to the way pasta was served: usually fresh, it was cooked (often in milk) until it was very soft and mushy, and flavored with sugar and other sweet spices. Gradually, dried pasta and the Neapolitan *al dente* way of cooking it became more popular and seemed to be more in syntony with the simplicity of its ingredients. Some colored pastas belong to regional traditions. Apart from Sardinian *malloreddus*, there are also green, spinach *tagliatelle* from Emilia, and *garganelli* from Romagna, which are flavored with nutmeg and grated lemon zest. On the whole, these types of pasta should be served either with simple sauces with an oil, butter, or cheese base, or with nothing at all, in order not to kill the flavor and to avoid clashing tastes.

Above: Top – trinette; Center: mafaldine; Bottom – tagliatelle.

Below: A vast range of common pasta shapes are also flavored with spinach, basil, tomato, porcini mushrooms, chillies, or squid's ink. Some even contain salmon, beet root, blueberries, or cocoa! Very often, both the consistency and taste of these types of pasta are fairly disappointing.

Fresh and Filled Pasta

Most fresh pasta is produced at home or in small quantities in tiny factories or laboratories (often in the back of a shop) for the local trade. The spread of fresh pasta since the 14th century is shown by the number of small fresh or semi-dried pasta manufacturers known as *lasagnari, vermicellari,* or *fidelari,* throughout the peninsula, especially in northern and central Italy. Experimenting with shapes and fillings, and combinations of these and with different sauces, local artisans have created the huge variety of fresh pasta now available in the various regions.

With few exceptions, fresh pasta is made from soft wheat flour, water, eggs, and a little salt. Sometimes bran flour or a mix of both flours is used. The dough must not contain more than 30 percent water. The use of eggs, limited at first, has gradually increased, so that it now almost totally replaces water. The addition of egg has increased fresh pasta's nutritional value and its calorie count: $3^{1}/_{2}$ oz (100 g) of egg pasta contains 370 calories, compared to the 356 calories contained in ordinary dried pasta. Sometimes just the egg yolks are used, and in some recipes, for example in Piedmontese *tajarin,* up to 20 egg yolks are used for each pound of flour! Although fresh pasta is eaten almost immediately, it does undergo a short drying period, known as *"incartamento."*

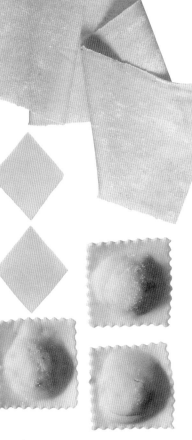

Above: Lasagne, maltagliati, and agnolotti.

Below: Homemade tortellini.

13

Stuffed pasta, one of the best-loved dishes in Italian cuisine, originated with fresh pasta. It has been considered the best and most refined type of pasta since Renaissance times. The richest array of tastes and consistencies have been married to the delicacy of fresh pasta, as the infinite variety of regional specialities and different stuffings demonstrate. *Agnolotti, anolini, cappelletti, ravioli, ravioli nudi, tortelli, tortellini,* and *tortelloni*: the repertoire of filled pasta is as rich and distinctive as that of dried and fresh pasta and is one of the highlights of Italian regional cuisine.

Making Fresh Pasta

M aking fresh pasta at home is a rewarding experience. It can be made by hand or using a machine.

Plain pasta dough
(Serves 4)
- 14 oz/450 g all-purpose flour
- 3 medium eggs
- ½ tsp salt

1 Sift the flour and salt into a mound on a clean work surface. Make a hollow in the center and break the eggs into it one by one.

2 Using a fork, gradually mix the eggs into the flour. Be careful not to break the wall of flour or the eggs will run. Continue until all the flour has been incorporated.

3 At a certain point the dough will be too thick to mix with a fork. Use your hands to shape it into a ball. It should be smooth and not too sticky.

4 Knead the dough by pushing downward and forward on the ball of pasta with the heel of your palm. Fold the dough in half, give it a quarter-turn, and repeat the process. Knead for about 10 minutes.

5 Set the kneaded dough aside for 15–20 minutes to rest. To roll the pasta by hand, flour a clean work surface and place a rolling pin on the top of the ball. Push outward from the center.

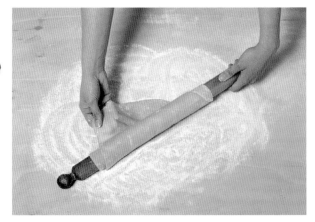

6 When the dough is about ¼ in (6 mm) thick, curl the far edge of the dough around the pin and gently stretch it as you roll it onto the pin. Unroll and repeat until the dough is almost transparent.

Spinach pasta dough

Proceed as for Plain pasta dough, working the spinach into the flour with the eggs.

- 8 oz/250 g all-purpose flour
- 5 oz/150 g cooked spinach, finely chopped
- 2 large eggs
- $^1/_2$ tsp salt

7 To cut the pasta by hand, fold the sheet of dough loosely into a flat roll. Use a sharp knife to cut the roll into $^1/_8$-in (3-mm) slices for tagliolini, $^1/_4$-in (6-mm) slices for fettuccine, $^1/_2$-in (1-cm) slices for tagliatelle, or $^3/_4$-in (2-cm) slices for pappardelle. Unravel the strips of pasta and lay them on a clean cloth. To make lasagne, cut the dough into 3x12-in (8x30-cm) sheets. To make maltagliati, roll the dough in strips about 2 in (5 cm) wide and cut into diamond shapes. Paglia e fieno pasta for 4 servings is made with one half quantity each of plain fettuccine and spinach fettuccine.

Using the pasta machine

1 To roll the dough using a pasta machine, divide it into several pieces and flatten them by hand. Set the machine with its rollers at the widest, and run each piece of pasta through the machine. Reduce the rollers' width by one notch and repeat. Continue until all the pasta has gone through the machine at the thinnest setting.

2 Cut the pieces of rolled pasta into sheets about 12 in (30 cm) long. Attach the cutters to the pasta machine and set it at the widths given for the various types of pasta. Lay the cut pasta out on clean cloths to dry for 2 hours before use.

Making Tortellini

1 (Below) Cut the rolled dough into sheets about 2 in (5 cm) wide. Cut them in squares.

2 (Right) Place teaspoonfuls of the filling mixture at the center of each. Moisten the edges of the pasta with a little water and fold over into a triangular shape.

3 (Right) Fold the top of the triangle over and pull the edges around to meet. Pinch the edges together and seal them. Lay the filled pasta out on clean cloths for 2 hours before use.

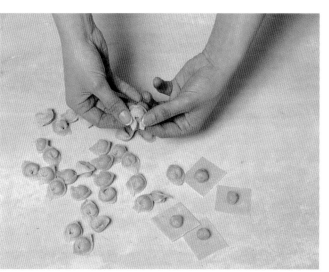

Making Ravioli, Agnolotti, or Tortelli

1 (Right) Cut the rolled dough into sheets about 4 in (10 cm) wide. Place teaspoonfuls of filling at intervals of about 2 in (5 cm) down the center.

2 (Left) Moisten the edges of the dough with a little water and fold it over to seal. Press down lightly between the mounds of filling.

3 (Below) Use a sharp knife or wheel cutter (the latter will give your pasta fluted edges) to cut between the mounds. If using a wheel cutter, roll it around the other sides so that they are attractively fluted too. Lay the filled pasta out on clean cloths for 2 hours before use.

Bigoli

Ingredients
- 14 oz/450 g whole-wheat flour
- salt to taste
- 4 eggs
- 4 tbsp cold water

Sift the flour and salt into a mound on a pastry slab or into a large mixing bowl. Make a well in the center and break the eggs into it. Stir with a fork, gradually incorporating the flour and adding water a little at a time, as needed. The dough should be smooth and elastic. Cover the bowl with a damp cloth and leave to stand for 30 minutes. Make the thick spaghetti-shaped bigoli using an electric or hand-cranked pasta machine.

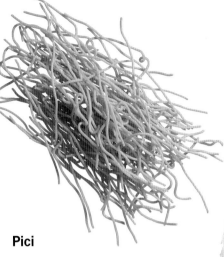

Pizzoccheri

Ingredients
- 11 oz/300 g buckwheat flour
- 5 oz/150 g all-purpose flour
- 3 eggs
- ½ cup/125 ml milk
- 1 tsp salt

Combine the flours in a large mixing bowl. Add the eggs, milk, and salt and stir to obtain a firm dough. Knead on a lightly floured work surface until smooth. Set aside for 30 minutes. Roll the pasta out until about ⅛ in (3 mm) thick. Roll the sheet of pasta loosely and cut into strips ½ in (1 cm) wide and 3 in (8 cm) long.

Pici

Ingredients
- 11 oz/300 g durum wheat flour
- 1 cup/250 ml hot water
- generous dash of salt

Sift the flour and salt into a large mixing bowl and make a well in the center. Gradually add just enough of the water to make a very firm dough, working it in by hand until the dough is as smooth and elastic. On a floured work surface, roll the dough out to about ¾ in (2 cm) thick and cut into thin strips. Roll each strip between your floured palms, slowly drawing it out until it is very thin and resembles a rather untidy strand of spaghetti. Spread the pici out on a lightly floured clean cloth.

Crespelle

(Makes about 12 crêpes)

Ingredients
- 3 eggs
- 3 oz/90 g all-purpose flour
- dash of salt
- 1½ cups/375 ml milk
- 4 tbsp butter

Beat the eggs in a mixing bowl with a whisk. Sift the flour and salt into another bowl and pour the milk in gradually, stirring all the time so that no lumps form. Pour into the eggs and beat until smooth. Cover with plastic wrap and chill in the refrigerator for 30 minutes. Beat the batter again before using. Melt 1 tablespoon of the butter in an 8-in (20-cm) skillet. Place a ladleful of batter in the skillet. Rotate the skillet so that it covers the bottom in an even layer. Place over medium heat and cook until the underside is golden brown.

Use a wooden spatula to flip the crêpe. Brown on the other side, then slide the crêpe onto a plate. Add a little more butter, and prepare another crêpe. Continue until all the batter is used up. Pile the crêpes up in a warm place until ready to use.

Basic Recipes

This page has six basic recipes for pasta sauces, plus three other recipes which are referred to later in the book. The pasta sauces can be served with a wide variety of pasta shapes.

Beef Stock

(Makes about 3 quarts/3 liters)

Ingredients
- 2 lb/1 kg beef
- 2 lb/1 kg meat bones
- 1 large carrot, 1 large onion, 1 stalk celery, 1 leek
- 2 cloves (optional)
- 2 bay leaves
- 1 clove garlic
- 5 sprigs parsley
- 2 very ripe tomatoes
- 4 quarts/4 liters cold water
- salt and freshly ground black pepper

Rinse and peel or scrape the vegetables. If using cloves, stick them into the onion. Place all the ingredients in a large pot with the water over low heat. The water should come slowly to the boil and barely move throughout the cooking time. Season with salt and pepper. Add just a little salt at the beginning; you can always add more during cooking. Skim the stock during cooking to remove the scum that will rise to the surface at first abundantly and then tapering off. Cook the stock for 3 hours over very low heat. Filter the stock into a bowl, discarding the vegetables. When the stock is completely cool, place in the refrigerator. If you wish to remove the fat, it will solidify on the top and can be lifted off and discarded.

Bolognese Meat Sauce (Serves 4)

Ingredients
- 2 oz/60 g diced pancetta
- 1 medium onion, 1 stalk celery, 1 carrot, all finely chopped
- 4 tbsp butter
- 11 oz/300 g ground beef
- 4 oz/125 g ground pork
- 4 oz/125 g Italian pork sausage, peeled and crumbled
- 1 freshly ground clove
- dash of cinnamon
- 1 tsp freshly ground black pepper
- 2 lb/1 kg peeled and chopped tomatoes
- 1 cup/250 ml whole milk

Combine the pancetta, onion, celery, and carrot in a sauté pan with the butter and cook over medium heat until the onion turns pale gold. Add the beef, pork, and sausage and cook until browned. Sprinkle with the clove, cinnamon, and pepper. Stir in the tomatoes and cook over medium heat for 15 minutes. Add the milk and season with salt. Turn the heat down to low and simmer for at least 2½ hours, stirring frequently.

Tomato Meat Sauce (Serves 4)

Ingredients
- 4 tbsp butter
- 3½ oz/100 g diced pancetta
- 1 onion, 1 carrot, 1 stalk celery, all finely chopped
- 11 oz/300 g ground beef

- 5 oz/150 g lean ground pork
- 1 cup/250 ml dry red wine
- 1¼ cups/300 ml beef stock (see recipe left)
- 1 tbsp tomato paste
- 2 lb/1 kg peeled and chopped fresh or canned tomatoes
- salt and freshly ground black pepper

In a heavy-bottomed saucepan, melt the butter until it bubbles. Add the pancetta, onion, carrot, and celery and sauté over low heat for 10 minutes. Add the beef and pork and cook for 5 minutes more, stirring frequently. Pour in half the wine and, when it has partially evaporated, add one-third of the stock. Simmer until the liquid has reduced, then add the tomato paste and a little more wine and stock. After 10–15 minutes, add the tomatoes, salt, and pepper. Continue cooking over low heat, gradually stirring in the remaining wine and stock. When cooked, the sauce should be fairly thick. This will take about 2 hours in all.

Basic Tomato Sauce (Serves 8)

Ingredients
- 4 lb/2 kg fresh or canned tomatoes
- 1 large onion, 1 large carrot, 1 stalk celery, 1 clove garlic, coarsely chopped
- 1 tbsp finely chopped parsley
- 8 fresh basil leaves, torn
- 4 tbsp extra-virgin olive oil
- 1 tsp sugar
- salt and freshly ground black pepper

Sauté the onion, carrot, celery, and garlic in a skillet (frying pan) with the oil for 5 minutes. Add the tomatoes, parsley, basil, salt, pepper, and sugar. Cover and cook over low heat for 45 minutes, or until the tomato and oil begin to separate. For a smoother sauce, press the mixture through a food mill. Serve with all kinds of fresh and dried pasta, and potato gnocchi.

Spicy Tomato Sauce (Serves 4)

Ingredients
- 2 cloves garlic, finely chopped
- 4 tbsp extra-virgin olive oil
- 6 fresh basil leaves, torn
- 2 lb/1 kg fresh or canned tomatoes
- 1–2 fresh chili peppers, sliced
- salt and freshly ground black pepper

Put the garlic and oil in a large skillet (frying pan) and sauté over medium heat until the garlic is pale gold. Add the basil, tomatoes, and chili peppers. Season with salt and pepper and simmer for about 15–20 minutes, or until the oil begins to separate from the tomato.

Tomato and Butter Sauce (Serves 6)

Ingredients
- 3 cloves garlic, finely chopped
- 1 large onion, finely chopped
- 4 tbsp butter
- 4 tbsp extra-virgin olive oil
- 1½ lb/750 g fresh or canned tomatoes
- salt and freshly ground black pepper
- 12 fresh basil leaves, torn

Combine the garlic and onion in a skillet (frying pan) with the butter and oil. Sauté over medium heat until the onion is soft. Add the tomatoes and season with salt and pepper. Simmer over medium-low heat for about 25 minutes. Add the basil just before removing from heat.

Genoese Basil Sauce
(Serves 4)

Ingredients
- 2 cups fresh basil leaves
- 2 tbsp pine nuts
- 2 cloves garlic
- ½ cup/125 ml extra-virgin olive oil
- salt to taste
- 2 tbsp freshly grated Parmesan cheese
- 2 tbsp freshly grated Pecorino cheese
- 2 tbsp of water from the pasta pot
- pat of butter for serving

Combine the basil, pine nuts, garlic, olive oil, and salt in a food processor and chop until smooth. Place the mixture in a large serving bowl and stir in the cheeses. Add the water and butter and stir well. Serve at room temperature.

Béchamel Sauce (Serves 4)

Ingredients
- 2 cups/500 ml milk
- 4 tbsp butter
- 2 oz/60 g all-purpose flour
- salt to taste

Heat the milk in a saucepan until almost boiling. In a heavy-bottomed saucepan, melt the butter with the flour over low heat, stirring rapidly with a wooden spoon. Cook for about 1 minute. Remove from heat and add half the hot milk, stirring constantly. Return to low heat and stir until the sauce starts to thicken. Add the rest of the milk gradually and continue stirring until it comes to a boil. Season with salt and continue stirring until the béchamel is the right thickness. If any lumps form, beat the sauce rapidly with a whisk until they dissolve.

Short Crust Pastry
(For a 9-in/23-cm pie plate)

Ingredients
- 11 oz/300 g unbleached white flour
- 1½ tsp salt
- 4 tbsp butter, at room temperature, thinly sliced
- 5–6 tbsp cold water

Place the flour and salt in a mound on a clean work surface. Make a hollow in the center and fill with the butter and water. Rub the butter into the flour. When the ingredients are roughly mixed, transfer to a lightly floured work surface and knead until the dough is smooth and elastic. Flatten the dough with a rolling pin and shape into a rectangle. Fold the shorter sides of the rectangle inward, one over the other. Roll into another rectangle, working in the opposite direction to the folds. Fold the shorter sides of the rectangle inward again. Repeat the two steps once more. Roll the dough into a rectangle or circle, depending on the pan or pie plate you are using. The dough should be about ¼ in (6 mm) thick. Line the base and sides of the pan or pie plate and cover with plastic. Chill for 30 minutes before using.

Agnolotti

A Piedmontese speciality dating to the second half of the 19th century, agnolotti were traditionally made by hand and shaped into little half-moons which were filled with meat (often leftovers from braised or roast beef), rice, Parmesan, and eggs. They were usually made on Mondays to use up leftovers from Sunday lunch. The most authentic version contains three different kinds of meat: roast beef, roast pork, and roast rabbit. Nowadays, they are usually shaped into squares or rectangles, and the filling can have either a cheese base, for example Parmesan, Taleggio, or Ricotta; a vegetable base, such as spinach, chicory, or beet root; or herbs, like sage and marjoram.

AREA OF ORIGIN: *Piedmont*

TYPE OF PASTA: *fresh filled*

INGREDIENTS: *white, soft wheat flour, eggs, water, and salt.*

SIZE: *1–1¹/₂ in (3–4 cm)*

COOKING TIME: *3–5 minutes*

FILLING: *spinach, beet root, chicory, Parmesan, Taleggio, or Ricotta cheese; beef, sausage; rice; eggs*

SERVED WITH: *Parmesan and white truffles; butter and sage; tomato sauce; melted lard and sage leaves (Biellese)*

20

Regardless of shape and filling, agnolotti are usually small with a distinctive toothed border.

Agnolotti alla Piemontese

(Serves 4)

Ingredients

- 1 quantity pasta dough (see recipe, page 14)
- 2 tbsp extra-virgin olive oil
- 1 onion, finely chopped
- 2 cloves garlic, finely chopped
- 5 oz/150 g Italian sausage
- 2¹/₂ oz/75 g pancetta
- 2 cloves, 1 bay leaf
- 14 oz/450 g roast beef
- salt and and freshly ground black pepper
- 1 oz/ 30 g dried porcini mushrooms, soaked in ¹/₂ cup/ 125 ml warm water
- ¹/₂ cup/125 ml dry red wine
- 11 oz/300 g spinach
- 1 egg
- 6 tbsp freshly grated Parmesan cheese

Prepare the pasta dough. Heat the oil in a large skillet (frying pan) and sauté the onion and garlic until soft. Add the sausage, pancetta, cloves, and bay leaf and sauté for 5 more minutes. Remove from heat and chop in a food processor with the roast beef. To make the sauce, return half the mixture to the skillet, season with salt and pepper, add the mushrooms, and simmer for 1–2 hours. During the cooking time, gradually add the mushroom water and the wine to keep the sauce moist. Meanwhile, cook the spinach in a little salted water. Drain, squeeze out excess moisture, and chop finely. Place the remaining meat mixture in a large mixing bowl and add the egg, Parmesan, and spinach. Mix well. Prepare the agnolotti following the instructions on page 16. Cook the agnolotti in a large pot of salted, boiling water until the pasta around the sealed edges is *al dente*. Serve hot with the sauce.

Wine: a dry red (Barolo)

Bigoli

This pasta comes from the Veneto region and the area around Mantua, where it is also known as *bigui* or *pincinelli*. It takes its name from the hand-cranked machine, or *bigolaro*, through which the lightly kneaded dough is passed. The resulting long strings of pasta are grainy, solid, and about the same width as thick spaghetti ($^1/_8$ in/3 mm). The dough is traditionally made with either whole-wheat flour (for *bigoli neri*) or white flour and bran flour in equal parts (for *bigoli bianchi*), egg, and warm water.

AREA OF ORIGIN: Veneto, Mantua area
TYPE OF PASTA: fresh
INGREDIENTS: white, soft wheat flour and hard durum wheat flour, water, egg, and salt
SIZE: length 10–12 in (25-30 cm), diameter $^1/_8$ in (3 mm)
COOKING TIME: 4–5 minutes
SERVED WITH: in Veneto, bigoli are eaten with rovinazzi (pieces of chicken); duck; goose sauce preserved in oil; anchovy and onion sauce (a Good Friday dish); mushrooms; tuna. In Mantua, classic toppings are sardine sauce, and pancetta and haricot beans sauce.

LOMBARDY VENETO
Mantua

Many small pasta-makers in Italy still use the bigolaro. The dough is placed in the machine and then squeezed through a metal-holed cutter at the end, coming out in the spaghetti-shaped bigoli as the lever is cranked. The bigoli are cut into strands about 12 in (30 cm) long with a floured knife before being placed on a flat floured surface to dry. They can also be made by hand, as in our recipe.

21

Bigoli with Walnut Sauce
(Serves 4)

Ingredients
- 1 quantity Bigoli pasta (see recipe, p. 17)
- 3 tbsp butter
- 4 tbsp fine dry bread crumbs
- 1 lb/500 g shelled walnuts
- 1 tsp sugar
- $^1/_2$ tsp each ground cinnamon and nutmeg
- 3 cloves garlic
- $^1/_2$ cup/125 ml extra-virgin olive oil
- salt and freshly ground black pepper

Prepare the pasta. Heat the butter in a skillet (frying pan) and add the bread crumbs. Chop the walnuts, garlic, sugar, cinnamon, and nutmeg together in a food processor. Place in a bowl and stir in the bread crumbs, butter, and oil. Season with salt and pepper and mix well. Cook the pasta in a large pot of salted, boiling water until *al dente*. Drain well and place in a heated serving dish. Add the walnut mixture, toss carefully, and serve.

Wine: a light, dry red (Merlot del Piave)

Bucatini

AREA OF ORIGIN: Lazio, Naples area, Liguria

TYPE OF PASTA: long, dried, tubed

INGREDIENTS: hard durum wheat flour, water

SIZE: length 10–12 in (25–30 cm), diameter ⅛ in (3 mm)

COOKING TIME: 9 minutes

SERVED WITH: butter sauces; pancetta; meat; vegetables; cheese; eggs; fish (fresh sardines)

Bucatini look like fat strands of spaghetti. They are named for their hollow, tube shape; *bucato* means "pierced" in Italian. They are associated with one of the most popular dishes in Roman cooking, *Bucatini all'amatriciana*, which has a tomato, chili, and pancetta sauce and is served with Pecorino cheese. This dish, in turn, is named after Amatrice, a small town at the feet of the Laga Mountains, on the border between Lazio and Abruzzi. A very popular spaghetti festival is held in Amatrice every year on the first Sunday after August 15th.

Other long, tubed pastas

Perciatellini, foratini, tubed *fidelini,* and tubed *fide* are some of the other long, tubed pastas that are similar to bucatini. All but the *perciatelli* (also known as *ziti*) are thinner than bucatini.

22

Bucatini

Perciatelli/Ziti

Bucatini with Bread Crumbs
(Serves 4)

Ingredients
- ½ cup/125 ml extra-virgin olive oil
- 10 anchovy fillets
- 1 lb/500 g bucatini
- 4 oz/125 g fine dry bread crumbs
- 1 tbsp each capers and chopped black olives
- salt and freshly ground black pepper

Heat half the oil in a small, heavy-bottomed pan and add the anchovies. Stir until they dissolve into the oil. Cook the pasta in a large pot of salted, boiling water until *al dente*. Heat the remaining oil in another pan and toast the bread crumbs in it for 5 minutes. Drain the pasta and place in a heated serving dish. Add the bread crumbs, capers, olives, and oil and toss well, then add the anchovy sauce. Toss again and serve.

Wine: a dry white (Cirò Bianco)

Cannelloni

The first cannelloni were prepared by rolling a sheet of fresh lasagne around some filling. Nowadays, they are available as dried pasta. So long as the sauce and filling are moist, they do not have to be cooked before being filled and baked in the oven. From region to region, this simple tubular form, straight or slightly curved, has given rise to a remarkable variety of names: alongside the biggest filled cannelloni (1$^1/_4$ in/3 cm diameter, 4 in/10 cm long), there are also smaller versions ($^3/_4$ in/2 cm diameter, 2$^1/_2$ in/6 cm long) such as *gigantoni, maniche, tufoli,* and *occhi di elefante.*

Other cannelloni-type pastas

There are many smooth, hollow pasta shapes that are slightly curved and smaller in size than cannelloni. Too small to stuff, they are generally served in *pasticci* (baked pasta dishes), or in soups. These include large *cannolicchi, sciviotti zitoni, occhi di lupo,* large smooth *sedani;* and medium-sized *cannolichi, scivotti ziti, denti di cavallo, fischiotti, canneroni* or *cannaroni.*

AREA OF ORIGIN: unknown

TYPE OF PASTA: short, smooth, straight-cut dried

INGREDIENTS: hard durum wheat flour, water

SIZE: length 4–5 in (10-12 cm), diameter 1$^1/_4$ in (3 cm)

COOKING TIME: 15–20 minutes

SERVED WITH: rich meat-based sauces; vegetables, cheese and béchamel

Spinach and Béchamel Cannelloni

(Serves 4)

Ingredients
- 1$^1/_2$ lb/750 g spinach
- 16 store-bought cannelloni
- 11 oz/300 g fresh Ricotta cheese
- 8 oz/250 g freshly grated Parmesan cheese
- 1 egg
- 8 oz/250 g Mascarpone cheese
- dash of nutmeg
- salt and freshly ground black pepper
- 1 quantity Béchamel sauce (see recipe, p. 19)
- 1$^1/_2$ tbsp butter

Rinse the spinach and cook it in just the water left clinging to the leaves. Squeeze dry and chop finely. Place in a bowl. Boil the cannelloni for half the time indicated on the package. Stir the Ricotta into the spinach together with half the Parmesan, the egg, Mascarpone, nutmeg, salt, and pepper. Mix well. Prepare the béchamel sauce. Butter an ovenproof dish large enough to hold the cannelloni in a single layer. Fill the cannelloni with the stuffing and place them in the dish. Pour the béchamel over the top and sprinkle with the remaining Parmesan. Bake in a preheated oven at 350°F/180°C/gas 4 for 30 minutes, or until golden brown on top.

Wine: a dry white (Soave Classico)

Capelli d'Angelo

CAPELLI D'ANGELO

AREA OF ORIGIN: Genoa, Naples area, the Ciociaria (Lazio)

TYPE OF PASTA: long dried or fresh

INGREDIENTS: hard durum wheat flour, water

SIZE: length 10–12 in (25–30 cm), diameter 1/20 in (1–1.2 mm)

COOKING TIME: 4–5 minutes

SERVED WITH: butter, cream, and Parmesan; light sauces; light clear soups; in the Naples area, also used for baked pasta dishes

The many different types of very thin, long pasta have different names depending on their thickness and origin. Capelli d'angelo ("angel's hair") and capellini are the most widespread names. They can be bought either cut in straight lengths or wrapped in *nidi*, or "nests." This pasta shape is popular in all areas of high pasta consumption, including the Far East, although there it is usually made using other types of flour, especially rice flour.

Capellini with Brandy and Herbs
(Serves 4)

Ingredients
- 4 tbsp extra-virgin olive oil
- 1 medium onion, finely chopped
- 2 cloves garlic, finely chopped
- 1 lb/500 g capellini
- 1 tbsp each finely chopped sage, mint, rosemary, bay leaves, parsley
- 5 tbsp brandy
- salt and freshly ground black pepper
- 4 oz/125 g freshly grated Parmesan cheese

Heat the oil in a large skillet (frying pan) and sauté the onion and garlic until they begin to color. Add the herbs and cook for 2–3 minutes. Pour in the brandy and cook for 2–3 more minutes. Meanwhile, cook the capellini in a large pot of salted, boiling water until *al dente*. Drain well and place in the skillet with the sauce. Toss over high heat for 2 minutes, then serve.

Wine: a dry white (Pinot Grigio)

Types of capellini
Capelli d'angelo are often served in clear soups or bouillon. They are slightly thinner than capellini. Other names include *capelvenere*, *fidelini*, or *fedelini*, *sopracapellini*, *capellini fini*, and *bassetti*.

CAPELLINI

CAPELLI D'ANGELO

Add color to each serving by placing a sprig of fresh mint at the center.

24

Cavatappi

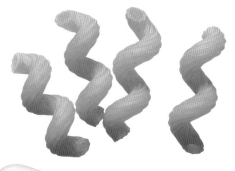

AREA OF ORIGIN: *northern and central Italy*

TYPE OF PASTA: *short dried, twisted*

INGREDIENTS: *hard durum wheat flour, water*

SIZE: *length 2 in (5 cm), diameter ¹/₈–¹/₄ in (3-5 mm)*

COOKING TIME: *10–13 minutes*

SERVED WITH: *meat, fish, and tomato sauces; vegetables and cheese; baked dishes; ideal cold for salads*

Along with other short, spiral-shaped pastas, such as *eliche, gemelli, tortiglioni,* and *fusilli,* cavatappi go equally well with meat, fish, or vegetable sauces and are ideal for pasta salads. They are also excellent when baked in the oven with béchamel or other sauces.

Cavatappi with Shrimp and Asparagus (Serves 4)

Ingredients
- 7 oz/200 g shrimp tails
- 4 tbsp extra-virgin olive oil
- 12 oz/350 g asparagus tips
- 2 shallots, sliced
- salt and freshly ground black pepper
- 1 lb/500 g cavatappi

Heat half the oil in a large skillet (frying pan) and cook the asparagus tips and shallots until tender. Season with salt and pepper. Heat the remaining oil in another skillet and cook the shrimp over medium heat for 4–5 minutes. Meanwhile, cook the pasta in a large pot of salted, boiling water until *al dente.* Drain well and add to the skillet with the asparagus. Add the shrimp and toss well. Serve hot.

Wine: a dry white (Vernaccia di San Gimignano)

25

A feast for the eyes
In recent years, an increasing number of colored pasta shapes have appeared on the market. Flavored with tomato, squid's ink, beet root, salmon, and mushrooms (among other things), they are attractive to look at but often disappointing to eat. It is probably best to keep them in a sealed jar on view in the kitchen and to use traditional pasta for cooking.

Conchiglie

Conchiglie, or shells, are also known as *arselle* or *gnocchi alla romana*. Available in many different sizes, they are all more or less densely ridged. The biggest conchiglie come from the Campania region. The smaller ones are from central Italy and various southern regions. They go by a variety of names: *conchigliette, tofettine, coccioline, cinesini, margheritine* ($^1/_3$ in/ 8 mm long); *tofarelle, mezze chiocciolette, cinesi, margherite* ($^1/_2$ in/1 cm long); *cocciolette, abissini* ($^3/_4$ in/2 cm long). The smaller ones require less cooking time (10 to 12 minutes), and are often served in clear soups.

The medium-sized types are also served in soups, or with tasty sauces.

AREA OF ORIGIN: Campania for the largest sizes; central and southern Italy for the small and medium versions; Campania and Liguria for lumache.

TYPE OF PASTA: dried

INGREDIENTS: hard durum wheat flour, water

SIZE: 1$^1/_2$ in (3–3.5 cm) long.

COOKING TIME: 14–16 minutes

SERVED WITH: light tomato sauces; vegetable sauces; Ricotta cheese; Genoese basil sauce

Lumache *or* pipe *come in just as many shapes and sizes as* conchiglie *and are served in similar ways. The larger sizes are sometimes filled and baked in the oven.*

LUMACHE/PIPE RIGATE

LUMACONI

26

CONCHIGLIE

Conchiglie with Artichoke Sauce
(Serves 4)

Ingredients
- 8 artichokes
- 4 tbsp extra-virgin olive oil
- 1 lb/500 g conchiglie
- 2 cloves garlic, finely chopped
- 3$^1/_2$ oz/100 g black olives
- 1 tbsp capers
- salt and freshly ground black pepper
- 2 tbsp finely chopped parsley

Clean the artichokes by removing the tough outer leaves and trimming the stalks. Cut in half and remove any fuzzy choke with a sharp knife. Slice thinly. Heat the oil in a large skillet (frying pan) and sauté the garlic until soft. Add the artichokes, olives, and capers. Season with salt and pepper and cook over medium heat. In the meantime, cook the pasta in a large pot of salted, boiling water until *al dente*. Drain well and add to the skillet. Add the parsley, toss for 2–3 minutes, then serve.

Wine: a dry, fruity white (Alghero Bianco)

Crespelle

CRESPELLE

Area of origin: unknown, perhaps 15th-century Florence

Type of pasta: liquid mixture of flour, milk, egg, butter, and salt

Ingredients: soft-wheat flour, egg, milk, salt

Size: 6–8 in (15-20 cm) diameter

Cooking time: 2–4 minutes

Served with: sweet and savory toppings; in stock; baked; filled like cannelloni or lasagne; with tomato sauce; meat-based sauce; Parmesan cheese, vegetables, and béchamel

Crespelle, the Italian version of crêpes, are made with flour, milk, egg, and a little butter. According to legend, they were invented in the Florentine Medici court during the Renaissance and taken to France by Catherine dei Medici when she went to marry the French king. There are a number of regional recipes for crespelle, including *scrippelle abruzzesi* (cooked in stock or baked), *cannelloni* from Campania, and sweet *palacinche* or *amlet* from Trieste and the areas near Austria.

Serving crespelle

Although crespelle are not strictly a type of pasta, they can be used in the same way as *lasagne* and *cannelloni*. Bake them in layers with a filling (cheese, vegetable, and béchamel), or wrap each crespelle around some filling and bake with a pasta sauce.

Rich Baked Crêpes

(Serves 6)

Ingredients
- 1 quantity crêpe batter (see recipe, p. 17)
- 8 oz/250 g ground beef
- 3 chicken livers
- 4 tbsp extra-virgin olive oil
- salt and freshly ground black pepper
- 8 oz/250 g spinach, boiled and coarsely chopped
- 4 tbsp butter
- 4 artichokes
- 2 tbsp finely chopped parsley
- 2 eggs
- 6 tbsp milk
- 5 oz/150 g Mozzarella, thinly sliced
- 8 oz/250 g freshly grated Parmesan

Prepare the crêpes. Sauté the beef and chicken livers in 2 tablespoons of oil over medium heat until brown. Season with salt and pepper and chop in a food processor. Sauté the spinach in the butter for 5 minutes. Clean the artichokes by removing the tough outer leaves. Cut in half and remove the choke with a sharp knife. Slice thinly and sauté in a skillet (frying pan) with the parsley and remaining oil until soft. Beat the eggs with the milk. Butter an ovenproof dish and line with a crêpe. Cover with a layer of meat, followed by a crêpe, a layer of spinach, another crêpe, a layer of artichokes, a crêpe, and a layer of Mozzarella. Repeat until all the ingredients are in the dish. As you work, sprinkle each layer with some Parmesan and a little of the egg and milk mixture. Finish with a layer of Parmesan. Bake in a preheated oven at 400°F/200°C/gas 6 for about 25 minutes.

Wine: a dry white (Bianco di Custoza)

Farfalle

Originally from northern Italy, between Emilia and Liguria, *farfalle* (butterflies) are named for their shape: a tooth-edged rectangle or oval of pasta, pinched in the middle. They range in length from $^{1}/_{2}$ in to 2 in (1 to 5 cm). Small farfalle, with a cooking time of 8 to 10 minutes, are used mainly in soups; medium farfalle, with a cooking time of 10 to 13 minutes, are served with pasta sauces or in soups; large farfalle, which take 13 to 15 minutes to cook, are served with sauces.

AREA OF ORIGIN: *northern Italy, between Emilia and Liguria*
TYPE OF PASTA: *short dried*
INGREDIENTS: *hard durum wheat flour, water*
SIZE: *length $^{1}/_{2}$–2 cm (1–5 cm)*
COOKING TIME: *13-15 minutes*
SERVED WITH: *tomato sauce; light sauces; butter and cheese; butter, cream, and peas; in salads*

EMILIA-ROMAGNA
LIGURIA

FARFALLE

Farfalle with Cantaloupe
(Serves 4)

Ingredients
- 1 small cantaloupe (melon)
- 1 cup/250 ml heavy cream
- $^{1}/_{2}$ cup/125 dry Port wine
- 1 clove garlic, finely chopped
- 1 lb/500 g farfalle
- 4 oz/125 g freshly grated Parmesan

Peel the cantaloupe and chop finely. Cook the cream, port, and garlic in a large skillet (frying pan) over medium heat for 5 minutes. Add the cantaloupe and simmer for 10 minutes. Meanwhile, cook the pasta in a large pot of salted, boiling water until *al dente*. Drain well and transfer to a heated serving dish. Pour the cantaloupe cream over the top and sprinkle with the Parmesan. Toss well, and serve.

Wine: a dry white (Albana di Romagna)

FARFALLINI

The smallest farfalle are known as farfalline, nastrini, nodini, cravattine, panierine, nocchettine, tripolini, stricchetti, *or* canestrini; *the medium ones are called* canestri, farfallette, stricchetti bolognesi, *or* modenesi, *and the large ones are called* farfalle genovesi, farfalloni, farfalle tonde, francesine, stricchetti tondi, saliere, *or* fiocchetti.

Fettuccine

Fettuccine and other ribbon pasta shapes, among the most classic types of pasta in the Italian repertoire, were developed from lasagne in the 15th century. They are ribbons or strips of pasta of varying thickness and width. In his book, *Libro de arte coquinaria* (c.1450), Chef Martino, cook for the Patriarch of Aquileia in Rome, suggests rolling sheets of lasagne up loosely and then cutting them "the width of a small finger" to get what he calls *Maccheroni alla romana*, nowadays known as tagliatelle. These are not to be confused with what Martini refers to as *Maccheroni alla siciliana*, which are a round, hollow pasta.

AREA OF ORIGIN: Lazio, central and southern Italy

TYPE OF PASTA: long, flat, dried or fresh

INGREDIENTS: white soft wheat flour, eggs, water, and salt

SIZE: length 10–12 in (25–30 cm), width 1/2 in (1 cm), thickness 1/20 in (1 mm)

COOKING TIME: 8-10 minutes for dried; 3-5 minutes for fresh

SERVED WITH: meat based sauces; tomato sauces; Italian sausage; mushrooms

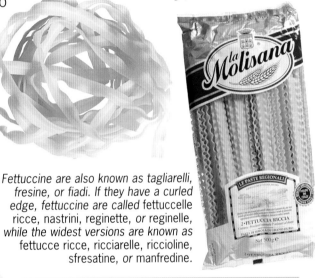

REGINETTE

For extra flavor, add a few chopped or torn fresh sage leaves to the butter.

Fettuccine are also known as tagliarelli, fresine, or fiadi. If they have a curled edge, fettuccine are called fettuccelle ricce, nastrini, reginette, or reginelle, while the widest versions are known as fettucce ricce, ricciarelle, riccioline, sfresatine, or manfredine.

29

Spinach Fettuccine with Butter and Parmesan
(Serves 4)

Ingredients
- 1 quantity spinach fettuccine (see recipe, p. 14)
- 4 oz/125 g butter
- 8 oz/250 g freshly grated Parmesan cheese

Prepare the spinach fettuccine. When they are ready to cook, boil them in a large pot of salted water until cooked *al dente*. Drain well and transfer to a heated serving dish. While the pasta is cooking, melt the butter in a small, heavy-bottomed pan. Sprinkle the pasta with the Parmesan and pour the butter over the top. Toss carefully but well and serve.

Wine: a dry white (Frascati)

Fusilli

AREA OF ORIGIN: *Campania*

TYPE OF PASTA: *dried, twisted*

INGREDIENTS: *hard durum wheat flour, water*

SIZE: *length 1½–12 in (4-30 cm), diameter ⅛–⅓ in (3-8 mm)*

COOKING TIME: *15–17 minutes*

SERVED WITH: *meat sauce, tomato sauce; Ricotta cheese; vegetables; seafood*

CAMPANIA

Torre Annunziata

According to legend, fusilli were invented in Torre Annunziata in Campania, by a person who thought of winding spaghetti around a knitting needle, creating what we now call *fusilli lunghi* (long fusilli). Before they were manufactured in factories, fusilli were made by rolling the dough out into a not-too-thin sheet, then cutting it into ½ in (1 cm) wide strips. These were then wrapped around little wooden sticks to give them their spiral shape as they dried.

FUSILLI LUNGHI

Baked Fusilli with Tomato and Mozzarella Cheese

(Serves 4–6)

Ingredients
- 1½ lb/750 g firm, ripe tomatoes
- 1 lb/500 g fusilli
- 4 tbsp extra-virgin olive oil
- 1 tsp dried oregano
- salt and freshly ground black pepper
- 10 basil leaves, torn
- 8 oz/250 g Mozzarella cheese
- 8 tbsp freshly grated Pecorino cheese

Blanch the tomatoes in a large pot of salted, boiling water for 1 minute. Scoop them out with a large slotted spoon and place under cold water. Add the fuslli to the boiling water and cook over high heat until the pasta is cooked *al dente*. Peel the tomatoes and chop them into small pieces. Heat the oil in a heavy-bottomed saucepan and add the tomatoes, oregano, salt, and pepper. Drain the pasta and toss with the sauce, basil, Mozzarella, and Pecorino. Place in an ovenproof dish and bake in a preheated oven at 375°F/190°C/gas 5 for 10 minutes. Serve hot or warm.

Wine: a dry red (Rosso di Capri)

ELICHE

Tightly twisted

Fusilli are often confused with eliche or spirals, which do not hold sauces as well. The long drying process required to give fusilli their shape adds substance and flavor to this pasta and makes them perfect for thick meat sauces or Ricotta cheese. Fusilli are also excellent for pasta salads, since they trap the pieces of tomato, olives, vegetables, herbs, tuna, and olive oil in their spirals.

SPIRALS

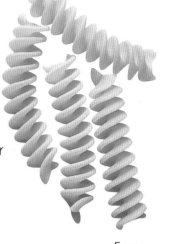

FUSILLI

Fusilli Salad

(Serves 4)

- 1 large eggplant (aubergine)
- 4 tbsp coarse sea salt
- 2 bell peppers, cut in strips
- 2 large zucchini (courgettes), thinly sliced
- 4 ripe tomatoes, chopped
- 13 oz/400 g Mozzarella cheese, diced
- $^1/_2$ cup/125 ml extra-virgin olive oil
- 2 tbsp finely chopped parsley
- salt and freshly ground white pepper
- 1 lb/500 g fusilli

Cut the eggplants in slices about $^1/_4$ in (5 mm) thick. Place on a large flat dish and sprinkle with coarse salt. Place a plate on top with a weight on it (a heavy book) and leave to drain for 1 hour. Rinse well and dry with paper towels. Grill the vegetables in a grill pan or under a broiler. Place in a large serving bowl with the Mozzarella and sprinkle with the parsley, salt, and pepper. Drizzle with the oil. Cook the pasta in a large pot of salted, boiling water until *al dente*. Drain and place under cold running water until cool. Dry well with a clean dish cloth. Toss well with the vegetables and serve.

Wine: a dry white (Pinot Bianco)

Garganelli

GARGANELLI

Area of origin: Romagna (Lugo di Romagna)
Type of pasta: fresh or dried
Ingredients: white soft wheat flour, eggs, water and salt
Size: length 2–3in (5–8 cm), diameter $^1/_4$–$^1/_2$ in (6–10 mm)
Cooking time: 10–13 minutes
Served with: fatty sauces (liver and giblet sauce); delicate sauces; almond sauces; butter and Parmesan; Scamorza cheese and courgettes (zucchine); peas, tomatoes, and cream

Garganelli come from Romagna, in central Italy. They are named for their resemblance to a chicken's oesophagus (a *garganel* in Romagnese dialect). They actually look like finely ridged macaroni, with the ends obliquely cut. The dough is made from flour, eggs, water, and salt, with the addition of Parmesan cheese, nutmeg, and grated lemon zest.

Homemade garganelli

These are made using a *pettine* (comb), traditionally two small parallel sticks held together by a kind of fine cane loom. A lightly floured square of pasta is placed on the surface of the "comb" and then rolled up into a tube around a pencil-sized stick, leaving pointed edges. By pressing lightly on the comb, the surface of the garganello becomes ridged.

32

Garganelli with Romagnol Meat Sauce
(Serves 4)

Ingredients
- 3 oz/90 g butter
- 1 small onion and 1 small carrot, finely chopped
- 2 tbsp finely chopped parsley
- 5 oz/150 g chicken livers, coarsely chopped
- 4 oz/125 g veal loin, coarsely chopped
- salt and freshly ground black pepper
- 4 tbsp dry Marsala wine
- 8 oz/250 g tomatoes, peeled and chopped
- $^1/_2$ quantity béchamel sauce (see recipe, p 19)
- dash each nutmeg and cinnamon
- 2 cups/500 ml beef stock (see recipe, p 18)
- 2 oz/60 g prosciutto
- 1 lb/500 g garganelli

Melt two-thirds of the butter in a large, heavy-bottomed pan and sauté the onion, carrot, and parsley for 5 minutes. Add the chicken livers and veal, season with salt and pepper and sauté for 5 more minutes. Stir in the Marsala then add the tomatoes, béchamel, nutmeg, and cinnamon. Cook on medium-low heat for 30 minutes, adding stock to keep the sauce liquid. Sauté the prosciutto in the remaining butter and add to the saucepan 5 minutes before removing from heat. Meanwhile, cook the garganelli in a large saucepan of salted, boiling water until *al dente*. Drain well and place in a heated serving dish. Pour the sauce over the top, toss well, and serve.

Wine: a dry red (Sangiovese di Romagna)

Lasagne

The Italian word *lasagna* has antique origins, deriving from the Greek *laganon* and the Latin *laganum*. A simple sheet of pasta, it is thought to have been the forerunner of the multitude of fresh pasta types that developed over the centuries. However, these older lasagne were served very differently. In a 3rd-century recipe by the Greek Athenaeus, in his book *"The Gastronomers,"* thin pasta sheets made from wheat flour and lettuce juice are flavored with spices and fried in olive oil. The *lagana* of the great 5th-century Roman cook, Apicius, was more like a meat pie than modern baked lasagne. It was not until the 14th century that the first lasagne similar to the one we know today appears in *Liber de coquina*, an anonymous book from the Court of Anjou.

AREA OF ORIGIN: northern and central Italy; southern Italy for curled varieties

TYPE OF PASTA: long, flat, dried or fresh

INGREDIENTS: soft wheat flour, eggs, water, salt; in Apulia and Basilicata: flour, warm water, and salt (no eggs); for the curled varieties, hard durum wheat flour and water

SIZE: length 4–6 in (10–15 cm), width $^2/_3$–2 in (1.5–4 cm)

COOKING TIME: 10–12 minutes for dried pasta; 3–5 minutes for fresh pasta.

SERVED WITH: meat sauces (liver, sausages); tomato sauce; mushrooms; vegetables; Parmesan and béchamel

33

Baked Lasagne, Ferrara-Style

(Serves 6)

Ingredients
- 1 lb/500 g store-bought or home-made lasagne (see recipe, p 14)
- 1 quantity Bolognese meat sauce (see recipe, p 18)
- 1 quantity Béchamel sauce (see recipe, p. 19)
- 5 oz/150 g freshly grated Parmesan cheese
- 5 tbsp butter

Prepare the pasta, if using the homemade type. Prepare the meat sauce. Prepare the béchamel. Bring a large pot of salted water to a boil and add 4 or 5 sheets of lasagne. Cook for 1 minute, then remove with a slotted spoon. Place under cold water to stop the cooking process, then place in a single layer on a clean cotton cloth. Repeat until all the lasagne is cooked. Butter a large ovenproof dish and line with a layer of lasagne. Cover with a layer of meat sauce, 2 to 3 tablespoons of béchamel, and sprinkle with a little of the Parmesan. Repeat until all the lasagne, meat sauce, and béchamel are in the dish. Finish with a layer of Parmesan and dot with the remaining butter. Bake in a preheated oven at 400°F/200°C/gas 6 for 20 minutes. Set aside for 10 minutes before serving.

Wine: a dry red (Sangiovese di Romagna)

Lasagne with Poppy Seeds

(Serves 6)

Ingredients
- 1 lb/500 g store-bought or homemade lasagne (see recipe, p 14)
- 3$\frac{1}{2}$ oz/100 g butter
- 1 oz/30 g sugar
- $\frac{2}{3}$ oz/20 g poppy seeds

Prepare the pasta, if using the homemade type. Cook the lasagne in a large pot of salted water until cooked *al dente*. Melt the butter in a small saucepan and add the sugar and poppy seeds. Drain the pasta and place in a heated serving dish. Pour the butter sauce over the top and toss gently. Serve hot.

Wine: a dry white (Müller Thurgau)

This unusual recipe comes from Trieste, in the northeast. It shows the influence of Austro-Hungarian cuisine.

LASAGNE

Size

Strips of lasagne pasta come in a wide range of sizes. Sometimes they are even cut to the size of the baking pan.

SPINACH LASAGNE

34

Curled edged and corrogated lasagne are typical of southern Italy and the Campania region. They are long dried pastas, ranging from the $\frac{3}{4}$ in (1.8 cm) wide curled "double" lasagnette (two pasta ribbons sandwiched together), to the 1$\frac{1}{2}$ in (3.5 cm) corrogated "double" lasagne, known locally as sciabò or sciablò.

The larger varieties of lasagna can be filled with meat, vegetables, and Ricotta cheese to make cannelloni. Otherwise they are served with wild game sauces and Neapolitan meat sauce with Ricotta cheese. They have a smooth and a curled side which picks up a generous amount of sauce.

LASAGNA FESTONATA

Linguine (Bavette)

Linguine (or Bavette, to use their Ligurian name) are flattened spaghetti from the ancient port town and financial center of Genoa. This city played a crucial role in spreading pasta throughout the Mediterranean. A major importer of wheat and dried pasta in the 12th century, 400 years later it was an important exporter of dried pasta. Old customs documents show frequent trading of pasta with Provençe, Catalonia, and central and southern Italy. The Historical Museum of Spaghetti, in Pondassio, Imperia, records the history of dried pasta production in Liguria. The museum was founded in 1824 by Vincenzo Agnesi, one of the first industrial pasta producers, who imported *Taganrog*, a hard wheat then considered to be the best in the world, from the Ukraine four times a year in his fleet of sailing ships.

AREA OF ORIGIN: Liguria

TYPE OF PASTA: long, dried, flat

INGREDIENTS: hard durum wheat flour, water

SIZE: length 10–12 in (25-30 cm), flattened cross section

COOKING TIME: 9–11 minutes

SERVED WITH: Genoese basil sauce; oil and aromatic herbs; butter; fish and shellfish sauces

Linguine are also known as lingue di passero, or "swallows' tongues." Trenette, trinette, or taglierellini are slightly wider than bavette.

Linguine with Green Beans, Potatoes, and Basil Sauce

(Serves 4)

Ingredients
- 1¹/₂ lb/750 g green beans, cleaned and cut into lengths
- 3 medium new potatoes, peeled and diced
- 1 quantity Genoese basil sauce (see recipe, p 19)
- 1 lb/500 g linguine
- 4 tbsp butter
- 4 tbsp freshly grated Pecorino cheese
- 4 tbsp freshly grated Parmesan cheese

Cook the beans and potatoes in a large pot of salted, boiling water until tender. Take them out with a slotted spoon and use the same water to cook the pasta. While the pasta is cooking, prepare the basil sauce. Add 2 tablespoons of boiling water from the pasta pot to make the basil sauce more liquid. When the pasta is cooked *al dente*, drain and place in a heated serving dish. Toss with the basil sauce, butter, and vegetables. Sprinkle with the cheeses, and serve.

Wine: a dry white (Riesling Sylvaner dell'Alto Adige)

35

Maccheroni

Sicily is undoubtedly the cradle of dried pasta, and macaroni are its first invention. From the 16th century on, however, it was the Neapolitans' taste for this pasta which decided its destiny both in Italy and throughout the world. Indeed, the Neapolitans (previously known as *mangiafoglie*, or "leaf eaters") were renamed *mangiamaccheroni*, ("macaroni eaters"), and in the 1800s, their city was dubbed the "Macaroni Capital."

AREA OF ORIGIN: Sicily, southern and central Italy (Campania, Molise, Basilicata, Abruzzi, Sardinia, the Marches)

TYPE OF PASTA: dried, hollow; many regional variations in size and shape

INGREDIENTS: hard durum wheat flour, water

SIZE: length $1^3/_4$–$2^1/_2$ in (4–6 cm), diameter $^1/_8$–$^1/_2$ in (3–10 mm)

COOKING TIME: 8–10 minutes

SERVED WITH: tomato sauce; pork or lamb sauce; sauces with chili pepper; baked dishes

Some of the more common regional types include: Maccaruna di casa from Sicily, Maccheroni della ceppa from the Marches, Ciufolitti and Maccheroni alla chitarra from Abruzzi, Maccheroni al ferro or inferrettati from the south, and Maccheroni bobbiesi in Emilia.

CALABRIAN MACARONI

MACCHERONI TRAFILATI CON BRONZO

36

Baked Macaroni

(Serves 6)

Ingredients
- 1 lb/500 g macaroni (any size)
- 1 quantity meat sauce (see recipes, pp. 18)
- 1 quantity short crust pastry (see recipe, p. 19)
- 1 quantity Béchamel sauce (see recipe, p. 19)
- 4 oz/125 g freshly grated Pecorino cheese
- dash of nutmeg
- dash of salt

Prepare the meat sauce. Prepare the pastry. Cook the macaroni in a large pot of salted, boiling water for half the time indicated on the package. Prepare the béchamel sauce. Roll the pasta dough out and use two-thirds of it to line a deep-sided 12-in (30-cm) baking dish. Drain the pasta and mix with the meat sauce. Place a layer of pasta and sauce in the baking dish and cover with a layer of béchamel and sprinkle with Pecorino. Repeat until all the ingredients are in the dish. Cover with the remaining pasta. Bake in a preheated oven at 350°F/180°C/gas 4 for 30 minutes. Serve hot.

Wine: a dry red (Carmignano Rosso)

History

Macaroni are first documented in the 13th century. Just 100 years later, "macaroni" meant any kind of homemade dried pasta. For example, the macaroni in Boccaccio's *Decameron*, in the story about the town of Bengodi, were in fact gnocchi. The term, of uncertain etymology, seems to have come from a variety of meanings just as size and shape still vary greatly from region to region.

MACCHERONI AL FERRO

Malfatti

Although the modern name for this pasta, *malfatti*, means "badly made," all the early authors of cook books and texts on gastronomy insist that the pasta for ravioli should be as thin as possible. Some even went so far as to suggest that the best pasta was no pasta at all! Salimbene da Parma, in his accounts of the late-13th century, viewed this trend as a sign of refinement and good taste. Chef Martini also recommended that the ravioli wrapping be extremely delicate, so thin, in fact, as to be almost invisible but for a fine veil of flour. *"Ravioli bianchi,"* or *raviolos sine crusta de pasta*, already existed in the 13th century.

MALFATTI

AREA OF ORIGIN: northern Italy, Emilia-Romagna
TYPE OF PASTA: fresh
Ingredients: fresh and mature cheese, eggs, aromatic herbs
SIZE: diameter ³/₄ in (2 cm)
COOKING TIME: 2–3 minutes
SERVED WITH: butter and cheese; butter and herbs; tomato or rosé sauces

Although the earliest "malfatti" did not have a pasta covering, they were still called ravioli. The great Renaissance chef, Bartolomeo Scappi, gives a recipe "to make ravioli without the case" in his Opera dedicated to Pope Pius V. This delicate dish of refined culinary art, highly esteemed by Renaissance courts, was made with fresh cheese, Parmesan, eggs, aromatic herbs, cinnamon, sugar, and saffron.

Spinach Dumplings in Pink Sauce

(Serves 4–6)

Ingredients
- 1 quantity tomato sauce (see recipe, p. 19)
- 1¹/₂ lb/750 g fresh spinach
- 4 oz/125 g soft Ricotta cheese
- 1 egg and 1 egg yolk
- 8 oz/250 g freshly grated Parmesan cheese
- salt and freshly ground black pepper
- dash of nutmeg
- 3¹/₂ oz/100 g all-purpose flour
- ¹/₂ cup/125 ml heavy cream

Prepare the tomato sauce. Cook the spinach in a pot of boiling, salted water for 8–10 minutes. Drain well and squeeze out excess moisture. Chop finely. Mix the spinach with the Ricotta, eggs, nutmeg, flour, and Parmesan. Season with salt and pepper. Shape into walnut-sized dumplings. Cook them in small batches in a large pot of salted, boiling water. Scoop them out with a slotted spoon as soon as they rise to the surface and place in a heated serving dish. Stir the cream into the tomato sauce and cook for 2–3 minutes. Pour over the dumplings and serve hot.

Wine: a dry red (Chianti dei Colli Senesi)

Malloreddus

Malloreddus or Sardinian gnocchetti are a traditional Sardinian dish. They have been made at home by housewives since ancient times. Made from hard durum wheat flour, their shape was obtained by first squashing the dough by hand then pressing it against the bottom of a wicker basket, to give each piece its distinctive fine grooves. Malloreddus are usually flavored with saffron or other aromas.

SARDINIA

AREA OF ORIGIN: Sardinia
TYPE OF PASTA: ridged and tapered dried pasta
INGREDIENTS: hard durum wheat flour, water, saffron
SIZE: length 4–8 in (10-20 mm)
COOKING TIME: 14-16 minutes
SERVE WITH: tomato sauce; meat sauces (sausage, pancetta, lamb); Ricotta, Pecorino cheese

38

Malloreddus with Lamb Sauce (Serves 4–6)

Ingredients
- 1/3 cup/90 ml extra-virgin olive oil
- 1 onion, finely chopped
- 4 cloves garlic, finely chopped
- 2 tbsp finely chopped rosemary
- 2 lb/1 kg lamb, cut from the leg into bite-sized pieces
- salt and freshly ground black pepper
- 13 oz/400 g peeled and chopped tomatoes
- 1 lb/500 g malloreddus
- 4 oz/125 g freshly grated Pecorino cheese

Heat the oil in a heavy-bottomed saucepan and sauté the onion, garlic, and rosemary for 5 minutes. Add the lamb, season with salt and pepper, and sauté until nicely browned. Add the tomatoes, cover the pan and simmer for at least 2 hours. Cook the malloreddus in a large pan of salted, boiling water until *al dente*. Drain and add to the pan with the sauce. Toss well, sprinkle with the Pecorino, and serve.

Wine: a dry red (Cannonau Rosso)

Pasta-making in Sardinia

From the 13th century onward the only serious competitor to Sicily in dried pasta production was that other great Mediterranean island, Sardinia. Customs records in Cagliari from the 15th century show that significant amounts of pasta were exported to other Mediterranean ports. Visiting the island in 1812, Archduke Francis of Austria-Este wrote: "*In almost every house in Cagliari and its suburbs (and in all of Sardinia), you can see little mills, or wheat grinders turned by a donkey ... which produce flour. The women make Maccaroni and other famous pastas.... The pasta keeps well: they dry it under the sun.*"

LA CASA DEL GRANO

TRADIZIONALI
Malloreddus
MEDI
500 g

Maltagliati

Maltagliati ("badly cut") or Malmaritati ("badly married") are square or diamond shaped pieces of pasta cut into zig zags from a roll of fresh pasta. The smaller ones are served in clear soups, while the larger ones are served with sauces.

Regional variations

As with other simple pastas, there are numerous regional variations on the same theme. In Umbria and Abruzzo, *strengozze* are made with just flour and water and are about ¹/₂ in (1 cm) wide and 4 in (10 cm) long. They are served with truffles, asparagus, or tomato sauces. *taccozze* or *tacconi* (2x2 in/5x5 cm) from Molise and Campania are also made with flour and water, while *pizzelle* from Puglia are prepared with hard durum wheat flour and salty water. Finally, in Liguria, there are *mandilli de sea*, thin 5 in (13 cm) squares served with Genoese pesto, and meat, or mushroom sauces.

MALTAGLIATI

AREA OF ORIGIN: *Emilia Romagna, Lombardy, Piedmont; central Italy (no eggs)*

TYPE OF PASTA: *fresh*

INGREDIENTS: *white soft wheat flour, eggs, water, salt*

SIZE: *irregularly shaped diamonds or squares, (2¹/₂–3 in (6-8 cm) long*

COOKING TIME: *4-6 minutes*

SERVE WITH: *light meat sauces; tomato sauce; stock for the small sizes*

Maltagliati with Beans
(Serves 4–6)

Ingredients
• 1 quantity maltagliati (see recipe, p 14)
• 2 oz/60 g lard
• 1 clove garlic, peeled but whole
• 2 tbsp finely chopped parsley
• 1 onion, 1 stalk celery, finely chopped
• 3 potatoes and 1 carrot, coarsely chopped
• 13 oz/400 g fresh cannellini beans (or presoaked dried beans)
• 13 oz/400 g peeled and chopped tomatoes
• salt
• freshly grated Parmesan cheese

Prepare the pasta. Melt the lard in a heavy-bottomed pan and sauté the garlic and parsley. Discard the garlic when it begins to color. Add the onion, celery, potatoes, and carrot and sauté for 5 minutes. Add the beans, tomatoes, and enough cold water to cover. Cook for about 1 hour, or until the beans are almost tender. Season with salt and add the pasta. Serve when the pasta is cooked *al dente*.

Wine: a dry white (Frascati Superiore)

Orecchiette

AREA OF ORIGIN: Apulia

TYPE OF PASTA: round, dried pasta, slightly dented in the middle.

INGREDIENTS: white or whole-wheat hard wheat flour, water, salt

SIZE: 1 in (2.5 cm) diameter

COOKING TIME: 14–16 minutes

SERVED WITH: vegetable sauces; lamb sauces; mushrooms; Ricotta cheese

Orecchiette come from Apulia, where they have been made for centuries, although food historians think they may originally have come from Provence, in France (the only center of dried pasta production outside of Italy). A similar pasta, called *crosets provenzal*, was produced in Provençe during the Middle Ages. A relatively thick pasta, it was cut into disks of varying size and pressed in the middle with the thumb to make the distinctive *orecchietta* (little ear) shape. Some sources credit the counts of Provence who, ruling from the court of Anjou at Naples, conquered Apulia in the 13th century, with introducing this pasta.

A sauce made with flowering turnip tops is perhaps the most traditional ways of serving this pasta. But cauliflower and broccoli are also popular. In Altamura, they are also served with mushrooms and sausages, or meat sauce.

40

Orecchiette are shaped like little hats with a brim. The dough is shaped into 12-in (30-cm) long sausages about the width of a finger. These are cut into 1/2-in (1-cm) chunks with a handleless knife, and dragged against a pastry board with a deft flick of the hand, to make the little inside-out shells. Even today, in the narrow streets of the poorer areas of Apulian cities, women can still be seen busily producing orecchiette for their families and to sell.

Orecchiette with Broccoli (Serves 4)

- 1 lb/500 g fresh broccoli
- 2 cloves garlic, finely chopped
- 4 tbsp extra-virgin olive oil
- 1–2 spicy, red chili peppers, thinly sliced
- salt
- 1 lb/500 g orecchiette
- 8 oz/250 g freshly grated Pecorino cheese

Trim the broccoli stem and dice into small cubes. Divide the broccoli heads into small florets. Boil the stem and florets in a large pot of salted water for about 8 minutes, or until tender. Drain the broccoli, reserving the water to cook the pasta. In a large skillet (frying pan), sauté the garlic in the oil until pale gold. Add the broccoli and chili, season with salt, and cook over low heat for 5 minutes. Remove from heat. Meanwhile, bring the water used to cook the broccoli back to a boil, add the pasta, and cook until *al dente*. Drain, and add to the skillet. Toss over high heat for 1–2 minutes. Remove from heat, sprinkle with the Pecorino, and serve.

Wine: a dry red (San Severo Rosso)

Paglia e Fieno

Paglia e fieno, literally "straw and hay," are a mixture of plain egg tagliatelle and green spinach tagliatelle. Green tagliatelle are probably the oldest type of colored pasta. They are made by adding lots of finely chopped cooked spinach to the basic flour and egg dough (see our recipe, page 15).

(see our recipe, page 15)

AREA OF ORIGIN: northern Italy, Emilia-Romagna

TYPE OF PASTA: long fresh

INGREDIENTS: white soft wheat flour, eggs, water, salt, spinach

SIZE: length 10–12 in (25–30 cm), wound up into nests or coils; width 1/4 in (6 mm)

COOKING TIME: 4–6 minutes

SERVED WITH: meat-based sauces and tomato sauce; butter or Mascarpone; Parmesan; liver sauces; cream and peas; ham; mushrooms

Paglia e Fieno with Peas, Ham, and Cream
(Serves 4)

Ingredients
- 1/2 quantity each plain egg tagliatelle and green spinach tagliatelle (see recipes, pp. 14–15) or 1 lb/500 g store-bought paglia e fieno
- 2 oz/60 g butter
- 1 small onion, finely chopped
- 11 oz/300 g fresh or frozen peas
- 5 oz/150 g ham, diced
- 1/2 cup/125 ml heavy cream
- salt and freshly ground black pepper
- 4 oz/125 g freshly grated Parmesan cheese

Prepare the two types of tagliatelle, if using homemade pasta. Boil the peas in a small pot of lightly salted water until just cooked. Melt the butter in a skillet (frying pan) and sauté the onion and ham for 5 minutes. Add the peas and cream and season with salt and pepper. Cook for 5 minutes. Meanwhile, cook the pasta in a large pot of salted, boiling water until *al dente*. Drain well and place in a heated serving dish. Pour the sauce over the top and toss carefully. Sprinkle with the Parmesan and serve hot.

Wine: a dry white (Pinot Grigio dei Colli Piacentini)

41

Long ribbons of pasta are often wound up together into *nidi* (nests or coils). Paglia e fieno sometimes come in mixed coils, like the one shown right, or in coils separated by color that mix during cooking (left).

Pappardelle

Pappardelle are long, flat ribbons of pasta, usually about 1 in (2.5 cm) wide. They are believed to come from Tuscany, where they are used in many traditional dishes, although they are also popular in northern Italy and other central regions. The name is thought to derive from the Tuscan dialect verb "*pappare*" ("to eat"), referring to large plates of pasta served with meat sauces, particularly game.

PAPPARDELLE

AREA OF ORIGIN: Tuscany, Emilia, Veneto
TYPE OF PASTA: fresh pasta
INGREDIENTS: white soft wheat flour, eggs, water, salt
SIZE: various lengths, sometimes in a nest, width 1–2$^1/_2$ in (3–6 cm)
COOKING TIME: 4–6 minutes
SERVED WITH: rich meat sauces, including game; mushrooms; giblets

VENETO
EMILIA–ROMAGNA
TUSCANY

42

Size and serving
Pappardelle are generally wider than tagliatelle, although width varies according to region. They are largest in Tuscany, where the handmade types can be 2$^1/_2$ in (6 cm) wide. Excellent with meat, pappardelle are usually served with braised duck, hare, and wild boar meat sauces, although they are also delicious with tomato, vegetable, or fish sauces. Broken or chopped, they can be served in soups and creamy legume soups.

Pappardelle with Duck Sauce
(Serves 4–6)

Ingredients
- 1 quantity pappardelle (see recipe p. 14) or 1 lb/500 g store-bought pappardelle
- 1 small duck, about 1 kg
- 4 tbsp extra-virgin olive oil
- 1 carrot, 1 small onion, 1 stalk celery, finely chopped
- 1 tsp fennel seeds
- 4 leaves fresh sage, torn
- 4 oz/125 g prosciutto
- 1 orange
- $^1/_2$ cup/125 ml dry white wine
- 2 lb/1 kg tomatoes, peeled and chopped
- salt and freshly ground black pepper
- 4 tbsp butter
- 6 tbsp freshly grated Parmesan cheese

Prepare the pappardelle, if using homemade pasta. Chop the duck into 6 or 8 pieces. Heat the oil in a large, heavy-bottomed pan. Add the carrot, onion, celery, fennel seeds, sage, prosciutto, and orange zest and sauté for 5 minutes. Add the duck and cook for 5 more minutes. Pour in the wine and orange juice and cook until well reduced. Add the tomatoes, season with salt and pepper, and simmer over low heat for 1$^1/_2$ hours. Remove the pieces of duck from the sauce, setting them aside in a warm oven. Chop the sauce in a food processor until smooth and return to the pan. Meanwhile, cook the pappardelle in a large pan of salted, boiling water until *al dente*. Drain well. Stir the butter into the sauce and add the pasta. Sprinkle with the cheese and toss gently. Transfer to a heated serving dish, arrange the duck on top, and serve.

Wine: a dry red (Chianti dei Colli Aretini)

Pastine

Small thread and grain-like pastas appeared in the Mediterranean during the Middle Ages in the area under Arab influence, from Sicily to Andalucia. In the Arab geographer Al Idrisi's 12th century *The Book of Rodger*, these pastas are called *fidaws*: pellets the size of grains of wheat, that were dried out in the sun. They were made from hard durum wheat flour. In the 15th century, Chef Martino mentions *millefanti*, tiny balls of bread and flour shaped into rice grains, to be "dried in the sun or by the fire." In the 16th century, Bartolomeo Scappi records this same process, paving the way for a wide range of soup pastas, whose shapes would be multiplied by 18th-century Genoese manufacturers.

PASTINE

AREA OF ORIGIN: southern and central Italy

TYPE OF PASTA: tiny dried soup pasta containing gluten

INGREDIENTS: hard durum wheat flour, water; soft-wheat white flour, eggs, water, salt

SIZE: varies from $1/8$–$3/4$ in (2–20 mm)

COOKING TIME: from 5 to 12 minutes

SERVED WITH: vegetable or meat stocks; thick vegetable soups; soup with pulses; tomato soups; the larger varieties can be served with sauces

Neapolitan smooth or ridged ditalini (also known locally as avemaria, paternoster, caporelli or corallini) are ideal for thick soups with peas, beans, lentils, and small vegetables. Sicilian smooth or ridged ditaloni go equally well with vegetable soups or sauces.

Pasta and Bean Soup
(Serves 4)

Ingredients
- 11 oz/300 g dried cannellini or white kidney beans
- 2 tbsp extra-virgin olive oil
- 1 onion, finely chopped
- 1 clove garlic, finely chopped
- 1 carrot, finely chopped
- 1 stalk celery, finely chopped
- 1 sprig fresh rosemary, finely chopped
- 5 oz/150 g finely chopped pancetta
- salt to taste
- 5 oz/150 g soup pasta
- freshly ground black pepper

Soak the beans overnight in a large bowl of water. Drain and transfer to a saucepan with enough unsalted cold water to cover them. Boil gently for just under 2 hours. When the beans are very tender, do not drain them. Remove one-third with a slotted spoon and purée in a food processor. Return the purée to the pan and stir. Heat the oil in a skillet (frying pan) and sauté the onion, garlic, carrot, celery, and rosemary with the pancetta until lightly browned. Stir this mixture into the beans. Season with salt. Bring the beans back to a boil, add the pasta, cook for 5 minutes, then remove from heat. Leave to stand for 20 minutes. Quickly reheat and serve with a grinding of pepper and a trickle of oil.

Wine: a dry rosé (Lison Pramaggiore Merlot Rosato)

Soup pasta today

Nowadays, soup pasta comes in a huge variety of shapes and sizes, ranging from tiny to small. They are made from hard durum wheat flour or fresh egg pasta. Depending on their size, they are served in clear soups, minestrone, or bread-based zuppe.

TRIPOLINI/FIOCCHINI

DITALINI

ROTELLINE

TEMPESTINA

ANELLI SICILIANI

CORALLINE

PUNTINE

STELLINE

FEDELINI TAGLIATI

QUADRUCCI

OCCHIO DI PERNICE

FUNGHINI TRINATI

Clear Soup with Pastine
(Serves 4)

Ingredients
- 4 cups/1 liter beef, chicken, or vegetable stock (see recipe, p. 18)
- 11 oz/300 g small soup pasta
- 4 oz/125 g freshly grated Parmesan cheese

Prepare the stock. Bring the stock to a boil in a large pot. Add the pasta and cook until it is *al dente*. Sprinkle with the cheese and serve hot.

Wine: a dry white (Soave Classico)

Penne

Penne, in all their varied forms, are the Neapolitan answer to macaroni. They have become extremely popular and have largely replaced macaroni on Italian tables. They are named for their diagonally cut ends, which recall the shape of the nib of old-fashioned ink pens. This same cut allows the pasta to pick up and hold a delicious amount of the sauce they are served with, which probably explains their popularity!

AREA OF ORIGIN: *Campania*

TYPE OF PASTA: *short dried*

INGREDIENTS: *hard durum wheat flour, water*

Size: *variable, length 1–2$\frac{1}{2}$ in (2.5–7 cm), diameter $\frac{1}{4}$ –$\frac{5}{8}$ in (5–13 mm)*

COOKING TIME *8–16 minutes*

SERVED WITH: *tomato sauce; light sauces; Neapolitan meat sauce; Genoese meat sauce; meat or vegetable sauces; oven baked dishes*

LIGURIA

CAMPANIA

Naples

Penne with Peas, Pancetta and Onion
(Serves 4)

Ingredients
- 6 tbsp extra-virgin olive oil
- 5 oz/150 g pancetta, diced
- 4 medium onions
- 1 lb/500 g fresh or frozen peas
- salt and freshly ground black pepper
- 1 lb/500 g penne

Heat the oil in a skillet (frying pan) and sauté the pancetta for 2 minutes. Add the onion and sauté until soft. Stir in the peas and simmer over low heat for about 20 minutes, or until the peas and soft and imbued with the flavor of the onions. Season with salt and pepper. Meanwhile, cook the pasta in a large pot of salted, boiling water until *al dente*. Drain well and add to the skillet with the sauce. Toss briefly and serve.

Wine: a dry white (Bianco di Castel del Monte)

45

Serving penne
The larger penne shapes are good with meat sauces. Try them with Tomato meat sauce (see recipe, page 18). The smaller shapes are better with tomato or vegetable sauces. Try them with pesto (Genoese basil sauce; see recipe, page 19). When buying penne rigate (ridged penne), remember that the best pasta-makers make ridges on the insides of their penne as well as the outsides, so that they trap a lot more sauce.

A wide range of colored penne are available today. They look very nice but are rather difficult to combine successfully with traditional sauces. Spinach penne are probably the most versatile of the colored types and go well with most tomato sauces and many meat sauces too.

PENNE AL NERO DI SEPPIA
(WITH SQUID'S INK)

PENNE AGLI SPINACI
(WITH SPINACH)

PENNE COLORATE

PENNE AL PEPERONCINO
(WITH CHILI PEPPER)

Size and shape

Penne are either smooth or ridged, and come in a variety of sizes. The smallest are *pennine, pennettine,* or *pennuzze* ($1/4$ in/6 mm diameter, 1 in/2.5 cm long; cooking time, 8–10 minutes for smooth, 10–12 minutes for ridged). *Pennette,* also called *penne di mezzani* or *penne regina,* are slightly bigger ($1/3$ in/8 mm diameter, $1 1/2$ in/3.5 cm long; cooking time 8–10 minutes for smooth, 10–12 minutes for ridged). Classic penne, also known as *penne di ziti* or *ziti tagliati,* have an $1/3$ in/8 mm diameter and are 2 in/5 cm long (cooking time, 11–14 minutes for smooth, 13–16 minutes for ridged). *Mezze penne,* also known as *mezze penne zite* or *mostaccioli,* have the same diameter as penne but half the length, as their name (*mezzo* means "half") suggests. *Pennoni* (*zitoni tagliati, penne di zitoni*) and *penne a candela* are larger: $2 1/2$ in/6 cm long, 1 in/2.5 cm in diameter. The real giants, however, are *penne di natale* or *natalini,* which are only available in the smooth variety and which come from Liguria and not Campania. They are usually served in clear soups or in baked pasta dishes.

MEZZE PENNE

PENNONI

PENNETTE

PENNE LISCE

PENNE LUNGHE

PENNE RIGATE

Pici

AREA OF ORIGIN: *Tuscany*
TYPE OF PASTA: *fresh*
INGREDIENTS: *white hard wheat flour, water, oil, and salt*
SIZE: *length $3/4$–1 in (2–2.5 cm), $1/8$ in (3 mm) diameter*
COOKING TIME: *6–8 minutes*
SERVED WITH: *meat sauce; tomato sauce; sausage and mushroom sauce; bread crumbs toasted in olive oil*

Arezzo
TUSCANY
Siena
Montalcino   UMBRIA
Montepulciano

The simplicity that lies at the heart of Tuscan cooking is nowhere more evident than in *pici* or *pinci*, a type of thick homemade spaghetti that is stretched and rolled by hand. The dough is among the most basic for fresh pasta: white hard wheat flour, water, a little oil, and a pinch of salt. The pasta is quite firm and is flattened into a sheet up to $3/4$ in (2 cm) thick using a short rolling pin. Little strips are then cut off from the dough and *"appicciate,"* that is "made into pici" by hand.

Traditions

In the areas around Arezzo and Siena, an old expression for making pici is *filare i pici* (spin the pici), a time consuming task traditionally assigned to girls. In the beautiful hilltop towns of Montepulciano and Montalcino, *pici all'aglione* is a famous dish. It is a mixture of lightly fried garlic, dried bread crumbs, chili, and parsley. Pici are known as *ciriole* or *stringozzi* in Umbria, where they are served with *salsa alla ternana* (spicy chilies and garlic fried in olive oil), asparagus or mushroom sauce, and black Norcia truffles sauce.

47

Pici with Spicy Tomato Sauce

(Serves 4)

Ingredients
- 1 quantity pici pasta (see recipe p. 17)
- 1 quantity spicy tomato sauce (see recipe, p. 19)

Prepare the tomato sauce. Cook the pici in a large pot of salted, boiling water until *al dente*. Drain well and transfer to a heated serving dish. Add the sauce and toss carefully. Serve hot.

Wine: a dry red
(Rosso di Montalcino)

Pizzoccheri

With its strongly contrasted culinary traditions, Lombardy's cuisine is as diverse as its landscape. In the northern, alpine valleys, local cuisine has been conditioned by the ingredients available. Pizzoccheri are made from one part white flour, and three parts buckwheat flour. Nowadays, buckwheat has been completely replaced by maize and, in Italy, is only grown in Valtellina, Carnia, Trentino, and Abruzzi. The flour, which has a slightly dark and bitter quality because of residual fibers from the wheat's coating, was once used mainly as animal feed. Dishes such as *pizzoccheri, sciatt,* and *polenta taragna*, to which the tasty buckwheat flour adds a distinctive flavor, have helped bring the grain back into vogue.

AREA OF ORIGIN: Valtellina
TYPE OF PASTA: fresh flat
INGREDIENTS: buckwheat flour, white soft wheat flour, water and salt
SIZE: length 2 in (5 cm), width 1/2 in (1 cm)
COOKING TIME: 10-15 minutes
SERVED WITH: melted butter, Bitto cheese, potatoes, Savoy cabbage, beet root, sage

48

Buckwheat (Polygonum fagopyrum) is not a cereal, but an annual herbaceous plant, which produces small, dark, triangular grain. Originally from central Asia, it was brought to Europe during the Mongol invasions. It spread in cool, mountainous, regions thanks to its resistance to harsh climates and poor soil.

Homemade Buckwheat Pasta Baked with Swiss chard, Potato, and Cheese (Serves 4)

Ingredients
- 1 quantity pizzoccheri dough (see recipe p. 17)
- 8 oz/250 g potatoes, in bite-sized pieces
- 6 oz/180 g Swiss chard, cut in strips
- 6 oz/180 g Fontina cheese, thinly sliced
- 6 tbsp butter
- 2 cloves garlic, finely chopped
- 6 leaves fresh sage
- 4 oz/125 g freshly grated Parmesan cheese

Prepare the pasta. Cook the potatoes in salted, boiling water. After 5 minutes, add the Swiss chard and, when the potatoes are almost cooked, add the pasta. Drain the pasta and vegetables well. Sauté the garlic and sage in a small saucepan with the butter for 3–4 minutes. Butter an ovenproof dish and line with a layer of pasta. Cover with a layer of potato, chard, and Fontina. Drizzle with a little butter, and sprinkle with pepper and Parmesan. Repeat until all the ingredients are in the dish. Bake in a preheated oven at 350°F/180°C/gas 4 for 25 minutes, or until golden brown. Serve hot.

Wine: a dry red (Valtellina Rosso)

Ravioli

Ravioli, together with other types of pasta, including *fidelli*, *formentini*, *tortelli*, and *vermicelli*, are first documented in the 14th century, a period of rebirth in Italian gastronomic history. Their origins are unclear, but they may date as far back as the 13th century. According to some sources, Ligurian pasta-makers at the end of the 13th century were the first to fold a lasagne sheet, cut it into squares, and fill them. This method spread from Liguria to Emilia and the rest of northern Italy. In the 14th century, ravioli were still considered more as fried pastry than filled pasta. According to Chef Martino, however, from the 15th century on, ravioli were no longer fried but cooked and served in stock.

AREA OF ORIGIN: northern Italy, Liguria and Emilia

TYPE OF PASTA: fresh filled

INGREDIENTS: white soft wheat flour, eggs, water, and salt

SIZE: 2–3 in (5–8 cm) squares, rectangles, or ovals

COOKING TIME: 4–6 minutes

FILLING: spinach, beet root, artichokes, egg plants (aubergines), asparagus, peppers, Parmesan, Pecorino, Ricotta, Mozzarella, Scamorza; boiled or roast meat, ham; fish meat or fillets; eggs; parsley, basil, marjoram

SERVED WITH: butter and Parmesan; butter and sage; tomato sauce; meat sauce

49

Ravioli with Sweet Ricotta Filling and Meat Sauce

(Serves 4–6)

Ingredients
- 1 quantity fresh pasta (see recipe, p. 14)
- 1¹/₂ lb/750 g Ricotta cheese
- 2 tbsp sugar
- 2 eggs, beaten
- ¹/₂ tsp ground cinnamon
- 1 quantity Tomato and butter sauce (see recipe, p. 19)

Prepare the pasta dough. Wrap the Ricotta in muslin and hang over a bowl for 30 minutes to drain. It should be as dry as possible. Place the Ricotta in a mixing bowl with the sugar, eggs, and cinnamon and mix well. Roll out the dough and prepare the ravioli as shown on page 16. Prepare the sauce. Cook the ravioli in a large pot of salted, boiling water until the sealed edges of the pasta are *al dente*. Drain well and place in a preheated serving bowl. Pour the sauce over the top and toss carefully. Serve hot.

Wine: a dry rosé (Rosato di Gioia del Colle)

Ravioli with Meat Filling in Tomato Meat Sauce
(Serves 4–6)

Ingredients
- 1 quantity fresh pasta (see recipe, p. 14)
- 1 quantity Tomato meat sauce (see recipe, p. 18)
- 7 oz/200 g ground chicken
- 5 oz/150 g ground roast beef or veal
- 5 oz/150 g finely chopped ham or salami
- 1 egg
- salt and freshly ground black pepper
- 1 onion, finely chopped
- 2 tbsp finely chopped parsley
- $3^1/_2$ oz/100 g fine dry bread crumbs
- 2 tbsp butter

Prepare the pasta dough. Melt the butter in a skillet (frying pan) and sauté the onion until soft. Add the parsley, chicken, beef or veal, ham or salami, and bread crumbs. Season with salt and pepper, sauté for 3–4 minutes, then remove from heat. Place in a mixing bowl and stir in the egg. Roll out the pasta dough and prepare the ravioli as shown on page 16. Leave the ravioli to dry while you prepare the tomato meat sauce. Cook the ravioli in a large pot of salted, boiling water until the sealed edges of the pasta are cooked *al dente*. Drain well and place in a preheated serving bowl. Pour the sauce over the top and toss carefully. Serve hot.

Wine: a dry red (Bonarda dei Colli Piacentini)

CLASSIC RAVIOLI

HALF-MOON SPINACH RAVIOLI

RICOTTA CHEESE

The filling for ravioli often depends on the occasion and the religious calender. On "lean days," Fridays, and Lent, ravioli are filled with fresh cheese, which is sometimes mixed to a cream, vegetables, herbs, or either fish (ravioli di magro, Trentino) or sole fillets (Marches). On "meat-eating days," ravioli are filled with meat, usually pork, but also poultry, especially capon.

The shape of ravioli varies from region to region. They are usually square or rectangular, and of different lengths. There are also oval shapes, including "rotondi" (round), or half-moons, such as caicc or Lombard ravioloni della Valcamonica (4 in/10 cm long).

Rigatoni

Short, tubular, straight-cut pasta, rigatoni are always ridged *(rigato)*, as their name suggests. Their special size and shape make them ideal for rich sauces. While their exact origins are unknown, they almost certainly come from central-southern Italy, probably Lazio and Campania, traditional areas of macaroni production (from which rigatoni are thought to derive).

RIGATONI

AREA OF ORIGIN: central and southern Italy (Lazio, Campania)

TYPE OF PASTA: short, dried

INGREDIENTS: hard durum wheat flour, water

SIZE: length 2–2½ in (5–6 cm), diameter ½ in (1 cm)

COOKING TIME: 15–17 minutes

SERVED WITH: meat sauce; tomato sauce; also used in baked dishes and salads

Summer Pasta Salad
(Serves 4–6)

Ingredients
- 1 lb/500 g rigatoni
- ⅓ cup/90 ml extra-virgin olive oil
- 8 oz/250 g Mozzarella cheese, in bite-sized pieces
- 4 oz/125 g black olives
- 2 tbsp capers
- 2 cloves garlic, finely chopped
- 4 medium salad tomatoes, diced
- 8 leaves fresh basil, torn

Cook the rigatoni in a large pot of salted, boiling water until *al dente*. Drain well and transfer to a salad bowl large enough to hold all the ingredients. Toss vigorously with half the oil then set aside to cool. Add the Mozzarella, olives, capers, garlic, tomatoes, basil, and remaining oil. Toss well and chill in the refrigerator for 30 minutes before serving.

Wine: a dry white (Bianco di Custoza)

Size

Rigatoni vary in size depending on their region of origin. Among the smallest are *rigatoni romani*, also called *cannaroni* or *cannerozzi rigati*, *sedani rigati*, or *gnocchetti rigati*. These types are about 2 in (5 cm) long and ½ in (1 cm) in diameter. *Rigatoni classici*, *rigatoncini*, or *paccheri* are just slightly larger. The biggest variety are *giganti*, or "giant," as their name suggests, also known as *bombardoni*, *maniche*, or *tufoli rigati* (1 in/2 cm diameter, 2¾ in/6.5 cm length). *Millerighe* ("a thousand lines") or *maniche centorighe* ("a hundred-lined sleeves") are the same size, but more closely ridged. *Elicoidali*, known locally as *trivelli* or *tortiglioni* (½ in/ 1 cm diameter, 2 in/5 cm length) have diagonal ridges, which hold sauces even more efficiently.

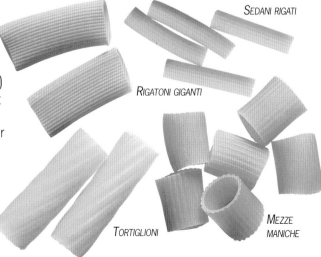

SEDANI RIGATI

RIGATONI GIGANTI

TORTIGLIONI

MEZZE MANICHE

Rotolo di Pasta

This is another variation on fresh filled pasta from Emilia-Romagna. A large sheet of pasta is covered with a layer of spinach and Ricotta, or a richer meat sauce, rolled up, wrapped in muslin, and boiled in a large casserole. It can be served sliced after boiling or baked in the oven with a sauce and served hot with lots of Parmesan cheese sprinkled over the top.

AREA OF ORIGIN: Emilia-Romagna
TYPE OF PASTA: fresh
INGREDIENTS: white soft wheat flour, eggs, water, and salt
SIZE: diameter 3–4 in (8–10 cm)
COOKING TIME: 20 minutes
FILLED WITH: spinach and Ricotta; meat sauces
SERVED WITH: butter and Parmesan; tomato sauce

Substitute the tomato sauce with melted butter and a few leaves of torn sage.

52

Baked Spinach and Ricotta Cheese Roll with Tomato Sauce

(Serve 4–6)

Ingredients
- 1 quantity fresh pasta (see recipe, p. 14)
- 1¹/₂ lb/750 g fresh spinach
- 13 oz/400 g soft Ricotta cheese
- 8 oz/250 g freshly grated Parmesan cheese
- salt and freshly ground black pepper
- ¹/₂ tsp nutmeg
- 1 quantity Basic tomato sauce (see recipe, p. 19)

Prepare the pasta dough. Cook the spinach in a pot of salted, boiling water for 8–10 minutes. Drain well, squeeze out excess moisture, and chop finely. Put the spinach in a bowl and add the Ricotta, 4 tablespoons of the Parmesan, and nutmeg. Combine well and season with salt and pepper. Lightly flour a clean work surface and roll the dough out very thin. Trim the edges to form a rectangle, about 12x16 in (30x40 cm). Spread the spinach and Ricotta mixture evenly over the top and roll the dough up into a long sausage. Seal the ends by squeezing them together. Wrap the roll tightly in muslin and tie the ends with string. Simmer the roll in a pot large enough to hold it lying flat for about 20 minutes. Prepare the tomato sauce while the roll is cooking. Remove the roll from the pot and unwrap it. Cut into slices about ¹/₂ in (1 cm) thick and arrange them in a buttered baking dish. Pour the tomato sauce over the top and sprinkle with the remaining Parmesan. Bake in a preheated oven at 350°F/180°C/gas 4 for 15 minutes, or until a golden crust has formed on the top. Serve hot.

Wine: a dry red (Collio Merlot)

Spaghetti

Without doubt, spaghetti is the most popular and best known pasta in the world, symbol of all things Italian. Yet spaghetti were the last type to appear on the crowded Italian pasta scene. Invented by the Neapolitans, the word first appears in a short 1824 poem by Antonio Viviani, titled, not surprisingly, *"Macaroni in Naples."* Long and cylindrical in shape, spaghetti were originally thinner, more like modern spaghettini or vermicelli. Later, when served with richer northern sauces, they needed to be thicker and consequently became the fatter spaghetti we know today.

SPAGHETTI

AREA OF ORIGIN: *southern Italy, Naples, Genoa, Liguria*

TYPE OF PASTA: *long, dried*

INGREDIENTS: *hard durum wheat flour, water*

SIZE: *length 10–12 (25-30 cm), diameter 1/12 in (2 mm)*

COOKING TIME: *9-11 minutes*

SERVED WITH: *garlic, oil and chili; tomato and meat sauces; vegetable sauces; cheeses; fish, shellfish, seafood*

53

Spaghetti with Seafood Sauce

(Serves 4)

- 11 oz/300 g each mussels and clams, in shell
- 11 oz/300 g each squid, and cuttlefish, cleaned
- 11 oz/300 g shrimp tails
- 4 oz/125 ml extra-virgin olive oil
- 2 cloves garlic, finely chopped
- 3 tbsp finely chopped parsley
- 1 teaspoon crushed pepper flakes
- 1/2 cup/125 ml dry white wine
- salt and freshly ground black pepper
- 1 lb/500 g spaghetti

Scrub the mussels and soak them with the clams in cold water for 1 hour. Chop the squid and cuttlefish into bite-sized chunks. Do not peel the shrimp. Put half the oil in a large skillet (frying pan), add the mussels and clams, and cook over medium heat until they open. Discard any that have not opened. Extract the mollusks from their shells. Leave just a few in their shells to make the finished dish more attractive. Heat two-thirds of the remaining oil in a large skillet and sauté the garlic, parsley, and pepper flakes for 2 minutes over medium heat. Add the squid and cuttlefish. Season with salt and pepper, cook briefly, then add the wine. Cook for 12 minutes, then add the shrimp tails. After 5 minutes add the clams and mussels. Mix well and cook for 2 minutes more. Turn off the heat, cover, and set aside. Meanwhile, cook the spaghetti in a large pan of salted, boiling water until *al dente*. Drain, and add to the pan with the seafood sauce. Toss for 1–2 minutes over high heat. Place in a heated serving dish and serve.

Wine: a dry white (Alicante)

Spaghetti with Crab Meat

(Serves 4)

Ingredients
- 2 cloves garlic, finely chopped
- 1 tbsp finely chopped parsley
- 4 tbsp extra-virgin olive oil
- 13 oz/400 g fresh or frozen crab meat
- 13 oz/400 g peeled and chopped tomatoes
- salt and freshly ground black pepper
- 1 lb/500 g spaghetti

In a large skillet (frying pan), sauté the garlic in the olive oil until it begins to color. Add the crab meat and cook for 2–3 minutes. Remove the crab meat and add the tomatoes. Season with salt and pepper and cook over medium heat for about 25 minutes, or until the sauce reduces. Cook the spaghetti in a large pan of salted, boiling water until *al dente*. Drain well and transfer to the skillet with the tomatoes. Add the crab meat, toss well, and serve.

Wine: a dry aromatic white (Müller-Thurgau)

Whole-wheat spaghetti is very good served with tomato sauce (see recipes, p. 19). It is also good with Genoese basil sauce (see recipe p. 19), and a variety of vegetable-based sauces.

TOMATO SPAGHETTI

WHOLE-WHEAT SPAGHETTI

SPINACH SPAGHETTI

Flavored spaghetti

Spaghetti is now also made in a variety of colors and flavors, including spinach, whole-wheat, tomato, chili pepper, nettle, and many more. Care should be taken in matching the flavors of the spaghetti itself with the sauce so that they don't clash. Traditional spaghetti is a vehicle for the sauce, whereas these newer types have their own personalities which must be taken into consideration.

SPAGHETTINI

Matching the size to the sauce

Spaghettini or *vermicellini* ("little worms" cooking time 5–6 minutes) go with light, tasty, or spicy, Neapolitan-style sauces. They are perfect with fish and shellfish sauces. *Vermicelli* or *fide* are slightly thinner than spaghetti (cooking time 8–10 minutes), and are probably the reason why a court chamberlain invented the four-pronged fork, in order that they might be eaten at the Anjou Court in Naples. They are excellent with fish, seafood, or vegetables. Larger types include *spaghettoni, vermicelloni* or *filatelli,* and *vermicelloni giganti.*

Spaghetti with Lemon, Cream, and Chili Pepper
(Serves 4)

Ingredients
- 2 lemons
- 1 clove garlic, finely chopped
- 1 cup/250 ml heavy cream
- salt to taste
- 3 oz/90 g freshly grated Parmesan cheese
- 1 spicy green or red chili pepper, sliced
- 1 lb/500 g spaghetti

Grate the zest of one of the lemons and cut the fruit into small pieces. Squeeze the juice from the other lemon. Sauté the garlic in the oil in a heavy-bottomed pan until it begins to color. Add the cream, salt, and lemon zest and pieces and cook over medium heat for 4–5 minutes. Add the lemon juice and cook for 2–3 minutes more. Meanwhile, cook the spaghetti in a large pot of salted, boiling water until *al dente.* Transfer to the pan with the cream. Add the chili pepper and Parmesan, toss well, and serve.

Wine: a dry white (Etna Bianco)

SPAGHETTI

Tagliatelle

Also known as *tagliarelle*, tagliatelle are long, flat ribbons of egg pasta about $1/4$ in (6 mm) wide. The narrowest ones, including tagliatelle, *tagliolini*, and *taglierini*, come from northern Italy (Emilia, Liguria, Lombardy, Piedmont), while the larger types such as *fresine*, *nastri*, and *fettuccelle*, come from central and southern Italy.

AREA OF ORIGIN: northern Italy, the narrowest in Emilia; the widest central and southern Italy

TYPE OF PASTA: fresh, long, flat dried

INGREDIENTS: soft wheat flour, eggs, water, salt

SIZE: 10–12 in (25-30 cm) long, often in nests or coils

COOKING TIME: 4–6 minutes if fresh; 8–10 minutes if dry

SERVED WITH: butter and Parmesan; cream with ham and peas; meat based sauce; tomato sauce; liver sauce; mushrooms; meat stocks

Tagliatelle are also produced in a variety of colors and flavors. Once again, while they look attractive they can be difficult to combine successfully with sauces.

PUMPKIN TAGLIATELLE

CHOCOLATE TAGLIATELLE

SPINACH TAGLIATELLE

BEET ROOT TAGLIATELLE

CARROT TAGLIATELLE

LEMON TAGLIATELLE

FRESH TAGLIOLINI

Tagliatelle are thought to have been invented in Emilia-Romagna. According to legend, they were inspired by Lucrezia Borgia's blonde hair and dedicated to her by the court chef in celebration of her marriage to Alfonso D'Este.

FRESH TAGLIATELLE

Serving tagliatelle

Traditionally, tagliatelle are served with a Bolognese sauce, made from a cut of veal rump, pork loin, diced Parma ham, chicken liver, and tomato, but they are also good with lighter sauces with a vegetable or mushroom base. In Lombardy, particularly in the Mantua area, they are often cooked in stock made from capon, whereas in the Veneto they are used in the regional *pasta e fasioi* (pasta and beans) dish.

Along with fettuccine, tagliatelle are probably the most popular type of of fresh pasta. Delicious and versatile, they are also the simplest to make at home. See our recipe on page 14.

Tagliatelle can be bought in dried form. They are made with egg, soft wheat flour, salt, and water, and then carefully dried so that they can be kept.

DRIED TAGLIATELLE

Tagliatelle with Leeks and Fontina Cheese
(Serves 4–6)

Ingredients
- 4 tbsp extra-virgin olive oil
- 7 oz/200 g leeks, cleaned and thinly sliced
- salt and freshly ground black pepper
- 5 oz/150 g Fontina cheese, diced
- 1 tbsp spicy mustard (optional)
- 1 lb/500 g tagliatelle

Heat the oil in a large, heavy-bottomed pan. Add the leeks and just enough water to cover them. Cook over medium heat until the leeks are tender. Season with salt and pepper, add the cheese and mustard, if using, and cook until the cheese has almost melted. Cook the tagliatelle in a large pan of salted, boiling water until *al dente*. Drain well and place in a heated serving dish. Pour the leek sauce over the top, toss gently, and serve.

Wine: a dry white (Erbaluce di Caluso)

DRIED FETTUCCELLE

Tortelli

Tortelli appeared at about the same time as ravioli toward the end of the 13th century and were derived from earlier medieval pies. Like ravioli, they were originally fried and their fillings were decided according to religious festivals and the liturgical calendar. Vegetable tortelli were not for people who could not afford meat, but were served on Fridays and Lent when meat was not allowed. They are thought to have originated in Emilia-Romagna and Lombardy (in the province of Mantua).

AREA OF ORIGIN: Emilia, Lombardy (Mantua)

TYPE OF PASTA: fresh filled

INGREDIENTS: white soft wheat flour, eggs, water, and salt

SIZE: varies, 2 in (5 cm) squares or rectangles, sometimes round in Tuscany

COOKING TIME: 4–6 minutes

FILLED WITH: spinach, beet root, potatoes, asparagus, pumpkin, Parmesan, Stracchino, Pecorino, Ricotta; pork or veal, ham; eggs; parsley, nutmeg

SERVED WITH: butter and Parmesan; butter and sage; tomato sauce; meat sauce

Potato Tortelli with Butter and Sage
(Serve 4–6)

Ingredients
- 1 quantity pasta dough (see recipe, p. 14)
- 1 ½ lb/750 g potatoes
- 1 large egg
- 3 oz/90 g freshly grated Parmesan cheese
- 3 oz/90 g butter
- 8 leaves sage, torn
- dash of nutmeg
- salt and freshly ground black pepper

Prepare the pasta dough. Boil the potatoes in their skins until tender. Slip off the skins and mash. Place in a mixing bowl and stir in half the Parmesan, the nutmeg, salt, pepper, and egg. Prepare the tortelli as explained on page 16. Cook the tortelli in a large pot of salted, boiling water until the sealed edges of the past are *al dente*. Drain well and place in a heated serving dish. Melt the butter with the sage and pour over the tortelli. Sprinkle with the Parmesan and serve.

Wine: a dry rosé (Carmignano Rosato)

Tuscan tortelli
Tuscan tortelli from the Lunigiana and Versilia areas are round (2 in/5 cm diameter) and are filled with beet root, Ricotta, mint, Pecorino, and eggs. The Tuscan version for "meat-eating days" are called *Tordelli in Garfagnana*. They are filled with minced pork, beet root, parsley, garlic, and eggs. Potato tortelli come from Borgo San Lorenzo, near Florence.

Tortelli di zucca

Tortelli di zucca (pumpkin tortelli), known locally as *blisgon* or *scivoloni*, are a typical Mantuan dish. They are tooth-edged squares or rectangles with about 2 in (5 cm) long sides, or half-moons. The traditional recipe for the filling includes cooked pumpkin, ground almonds, spiced apple mustard, nutmeg, egg, bread crumbs, and sugar if the pumpkin is bitter. There are many variations; our recipe is a modern one for busy cooks. Try adding 4 oz (125 g) of crushed Amaretti cookies for a sweeter filling.

The size, shape, and filling of tortelli varies from region to region (and also from cook to cook). Tortelli alle erbe (with herbs), from Parma, are served on the eve of religious festivals and on "lean" days. They are about 2 in (5 cm) square, and filled with sweet Parma chicory, Ricotta, Parmesan, eggs, and nutmeg.

Tortelli with Pumpkin Filling

(Serve 4–6)

Ingredients
- 2½ lb/1.2 kg fresh pumpkin
- 7 oz/200 g freshly grated Parmesan cheese
- 1 egg
- dash of grated nutmeg
- 2 oz/60 g fine dry bread crumbs
- salt to taste
- 3 oz/90 g butter, melted
- 1 quantity pasta dough (see recipe, p. 14)

Without peeling the pumpkin, scrape away the seeds and fibers and cut it into slices about 2 in (5 cm) thick. Bake in a preheated oven at 400°F/200°C/gas 6 until tender. Remove the flesh from the skin. Sieve the flesh into a mixing bowl while still hot. Mix well with three-quarters of the Parmesan, the egg, nutmeg, bread crumbs, and salt. Cover the bowl with plastic wrap and leave to stand for 2 hours. Prepare the pasta dough as explained on page 14. Prepare the tortelli as explained on page 16. Cook in a large pan of salted, boiling water until the sealed edges of the pasta are cooked *al dente*. Drizzle with the butter and sprinkle with the remaining Parmesan. Serve hot.

Wine: a dry or medium sparkling red (Lambrusco di Sorbara)

Tortellini

Legend has it that tortellini were invented by an innkeeper at Castelfranco Bolognese, a town midway between Bologna and Modena. Both cities claim credit for this delicious filled pasta, the shape of which is said to pay homage to the love goddess Venus' belly button. According to another version, is was the navel of a Bolognese Marquis' daughter that inspired their shape. Although no one really knows how they originated, by the 16th century, tortellini were a recognized Bolognese speciality. Skillfully made by hand, up until the 1940s they were only served in boiling stock at Christmas, New Year, and Easter. They became more widespread when the Bertagni brothers, pasta-makers from Bologna, discovered how to preserve them. As a result, in 1904 and 1906, tortellini crossed the Atlantic to be displayed at the International Exhibition in Los Angeles.

AREA OF ORIGIN: Emilia, Bologna, Modena
TYPE OF PASTA: fresh filled
INGREDIENTS: white soft wheat flour
Size: 1¹/₂ in (3–4 cm), triangle folded into a ring
COOKING TIME: 4–6 minutes (homemade)15–20 minutes (store-bought)
FILLING: Parma ham, mortadella, pork loin, eggs, Parmesan, and nutmeg
SERVED WITH: meat stock (beef, capon); meat or tomato sauce

60

Tortellini in Boiling Beef Stock
(Serve 4)

Ingredients
- 1 quantity pasta dough (see recipe, p. 14)
- 2 tbsp butter
- 4 oz/125 g lean pork, coarsely chopped
- 3 oz/90 g mortadella
- 3 oz/90 g prosciutto
- 1 egg
- 8 oz/250 g freshly grated Parmesan cheese
- dash of nutmeg
- salt and freshly ground black pepper
- 2 quarts/2 liters boiling beef stock (see recipe, p. 18)

Prepare the pasta dough. Melt the butter in a skillet (frying pan) and sauté the pork. When browned, chop finely in a food processor with the mortadella and prosciutto. Transfer to a mixing bowl and stir in the egg, Parmesan, nutmeg, salt, and pepper. Prepare the tortellini as explained on page 16. Spread them out on a clean cloth to dry for about 2 hours. Bring the stock to a boil in a large pan and add the tortellini. Simmer gently until the sealed edges of the pasta are cooked *al dente*. Ladle the stock and tortellini into individual soup bowls and serve hot.

Wine: a dry red (Sangiovese di Romagna)

Tortellini Soufflé

(Serves 4)

Ingredients
- 13 oz/400 g tortellini, store-bought or homemade (see recipe, facing page)
- 1 quantity Béchamel sauce (see recipe, p. 19)
- 4 eggs, separated
- salt and freshly ground black pepper
- dash of nutmeg
- 3 oz/90 g freshly grated Parmesan cheese
- $1/4$ cup/75 ml heavy cream
- 1 tbsp butter

Prepare the tortellini. Prepare the béchamel. Stir the egg yolks into the béchamel. Season with salt, pepper, and nutmeg. Cook the tortellini in a large pot of salted, boiling water until the pasta around the edges is cooked *al dente*. Drain well and add to the béchamel. Beat the egg whites until stiff. Stir in the cream and Parmesan, then fold in the egg whites. Butter a large soufflé mold and fill with the mixture. Bake in a preheated oven at 400°F/200°C/gas 6 for 20 minutes, or until golden brown on top. Serve hot.

Wine: a dry white (Bianco di Montecarlo)

Tortellini
Industriali

Other filled pasta specialties from Emilia

Emilia is also famous for *agnolini di Parma* and *cappelletti di Reggio*. Agnolini are scalloped rings filled with mature Parmesan (aged for at least two years), egg, bread crumbs, nutmeg, and salt. Cappelletti ("little hats") are very similar to tortellini in shape. Their filling consists of veal, beef, and pork, with bread crumbs and Parmesan. They can be served in stock, or with a meat or tomato sauce.

Tortellini are square or rhomboid with $1^1/_2$ in (3–4 cm) sides. They are then folded into triangles whose ends are joined together, creating a ring around the index finger. The filling, anma (soul) in Emilian dialect, consists of Parma ham, Bolognese mortadella, pork loin browned in butter, egg, Parmesan and nutmeg. The tortellini filling recipe was registered by the Italian Cooking Academy in 1974, and by the Dotta Tortellino Guild at the Chamber of Commerce in Bologna.

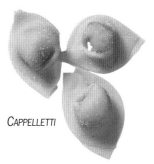

Cappelletti

Index

Credits

The Publishers would like to thank

Mastrociliegia (Fiesole)
Dino Bartolini (Florence)
La Boutique della Pasta Fresca (Florence)
who kindly lent props for the photography.

All photos by Marco Lanza and Walter Mericchi except:

Archivio Storico Barilla, Parma: 6т, 7, 8в, 9т, 10т, 11т
Buhler S.p.A., Segrate: 9в